SUMO

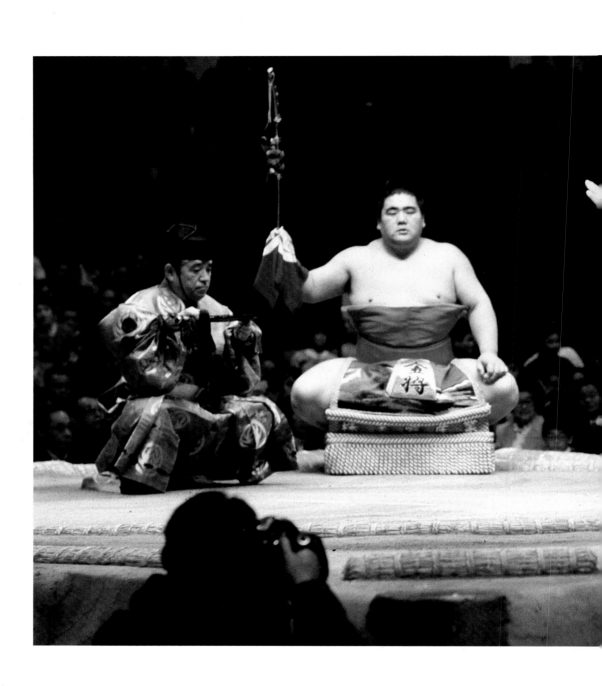

ANDY ADAMS
CLYDE NEWTON

SUMO

INTRODUCTIONS BY TOMOTAKA DEWANOUMI AND OZEKI KONISHIKI

PHOTOGRAPHY BY
GERRY TOFF

GALLERY BOOKS
An Imprint of W. H. Smith Publishers Inc.
112 Madison Avenue
New York City 10016

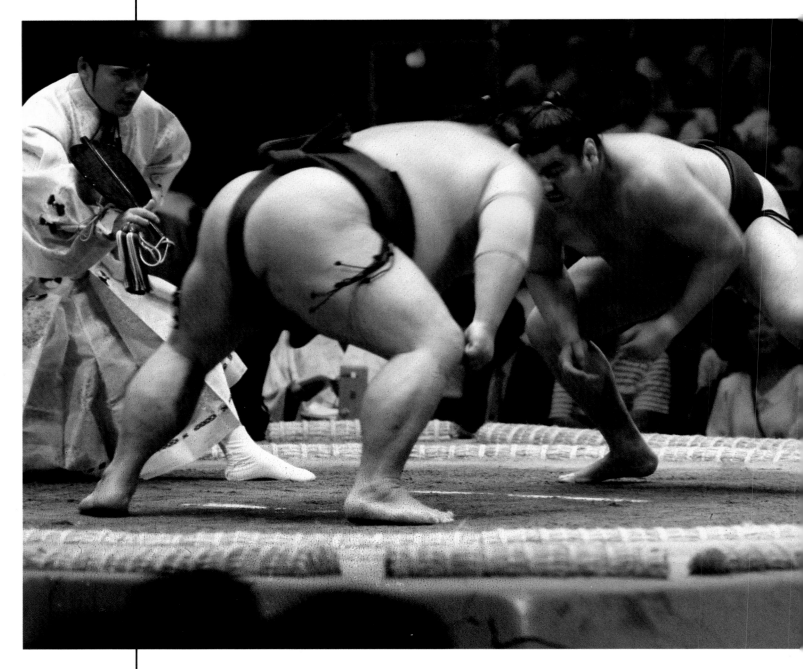

First published in 1989 by
The Hamlyn Publishing Group Limited
an imprint of The Octopus Publishing Group
Michelin House, 81 Fulham Road
London SW3 6RB

This edition published in 1989 by Gallery Books
an imprint of W. H. Smith Publishers Inc.
112 Madison Avenue, New York, NY 10016

ISBN 0 8317 7997 7

Produced by Mandarin Offset
Printed in Hong Kong

CONTENTS

INTRODUCTIONS

TOMOTAKA DEWANOUMI

The popularity of sumo in Japan goes back more than a thousand years, during which time sumo has continued to be one of the few truly Japanese sports. Over the past four hundred years many descriptions of it have appeared in Western writings, but only recently has any real attempt been made to understand and explain the intricacy of sumo and the appeal it has for Japanese of all ages, from the Emperor to the youngest primary schoolchild. Sumo's present appeal to audiences on Western television may be explained by the fact that, in spite of the colour and ritual, almost no emotion is shown after the bout by winners or losers, only the same extreme of politeness. For someone who has missed the actual bout it is often impossible to tell from the expressions of the wrestlers who has won or lost. When compared with the exaggerated poses of Olympic champions, tennis and football stars, we are suddenly brought back to reality.

I hope that this book, which has been written in the same restrained tones, will help to explain some of the finer points of sumo, and stimulate interest in the life and strict training that sumo wrestlers undergo. Sumo has a unique place in Japanese life and history, and deserves to be Japan's National Sport.

出羽海 智敬

Tomotaka Dewanoumi (formerly Sadanoyama, 50th Grand Champion)

OZEKI KONISHIKI

Japanese traditional sumo is really getting more and more popular around the world lately, not only with foreign fans but also with young guys coming to Japan and joining stables. Right now, there's about 20 foreign sumo wrestlers, not only from Hawaii, but even from faraway countries like Argentina and Britain. I understand there's a big sumo boom going on in Britain these days and that the Sumo Association is planning to hold a jungyo tournament in London in 1991.

Sumo is a way of life, even for a foreigner like me. To be honest, the first two-and-a-half years were hard, probably because I didn't love sumo the way I love it now. Now I know how the system runs and I understand the customs of sumo. To be a good sumo wrestler, you have to follow the whole range of customs. That's one thing I really learned. Now, I like the way the system is run. It's hard but it works. The people who go through the system and obey the orders given them are the ones who really make it. I love the system. It's harsh, but it's still a good way to straighten young guys out.

One of my favourite words in Japanese is *gaman*, which means perseverance. The big injury I had in 1986 was one of the turning points in my career. I told myself that it wouldn't stop me. Because of this, there's no way I'm going to stop: I'll keep doing sumo until I can't walk.

Ozeki Konishiki (Salevaa Atisanoe)

SETTING THE SCENE

Enter Tokyo's traditional Japanese sumo arena and you cross the threshold into a world as enigmatic and mysterious as the world of the geisha in their teahouse. Sumo is an ancient form of wrestling that combines tradition, religious ritual and man-to-man combat. Every afternoon during the six annual 15-day tournaments some 11,000 avid fans cram themselves into the straw-matted stalls and seats of one of the nation's four sumo arenas to experience first-hand the pageantry and excitement of one of the world's oldest and most colourful sports. Millions more watch the action on television.

Sumo flourishes in the tiniest villages too cramped to make room for a baseball field or too poor to outfit a team. To practise sumo, however, all a boy has to do is to don an improvised loin cloth and trace a large circle in the dirt. Now he's ready to start wrestling.

To most non-Japanese, sumo is intriguingly exotic, its moments of violent, spectacular action contrasting with the elaborate rituals that are central to a sport whose roots lie deep in Japan's Shinto religion.

The atmosphere inside Tokyo's National Sumo Arena, the Kokugikan, has a magic all its own. Overhead, the two-ton symbolic Shinto-style roof hangs above the ring suspended by cables. Behind the scenes in the changing rooms, the hair-dressers prepare the ginko-leaf-shaped hair-dos of the wrestlers in the two top divisions.

The referees, ring attendants and ticket-ushers wear colourful costumes of Japan's Muromachi and

A typical late afternoon scene at one of the tournaments. The two wrestlers, accompanied by the yobidashi, are going through the preliminaries of a bout. The seating nearest the ring is on individual cushions and is called *suna-kaburi*, literally 'sand-covered', for obvious reasons. These seats are for the real aficionados. Behind the rows of individual cushions are boxes, called *masuseki*, usually built to hold four spectators, who are also given cushions plus ample amounts of food and drink the price being included in the cost of the ticket.

Edo periods. The grand champions, bedecked in elaborate silk-embroidered aprons and huge white rope-belts, go through their own ring-entering ritual. The other wrestlers from the top two divisions parade down the aisle, climb onto the clay ring, then face outward and clap their hands in unison in other pre-bout ceremonies.

Sumo is not merely the national sport of Japan: it contains something of the essence of Japan. Japanese at a sumo tournament are more at ease, more themselves than at any other time or in any other place. Nowhere is their friendliness and conviviality more evident. They're truly in their element as part of the group while eating, drinking and watching the bouts, and at the same time they express their individuality by humorous repartee and the ways they cheer their favourites.

The pageantry and ritual that accompany the preliminaries to each contest make a striking contrast to the bout itself, which seldom lasts longer than 30 seconds. At the crucial opening charge, all that compressed energy and power is in-stantly unleashed, as the two mass-ive wrestlers hurl themselves at each other in a bone-shattering collision. All those years of gruelling training and building up a giant-sized body are packed into the few seconds of explosive action.

A tournament day usually lasts from about 10.30 in the morning to 6 at night, and fans will see 350 to 400 bouts on each of the 15 days of the tournament. The contenders are divided into divisions based not on weight but on tournament victories. Often a talented little 200-pounder will take on a wrestler twice his size – and beat him.

The wrestlers in the top two divisions fight all 15 days in a tournament, while those in the four lower divisions wrestle only on seven days. At the conclusion of the final bout of the day, a traditional bow-twirling ceremony is performed, while outside the arena, on a rickety, 50-foot-high scaffolding tower, one of the ring attendants beats on a small drum with his hands as the spectators stream out – witnesses to an exhilarating event in which Japan's past and present are one.

One of the head re-ferees reads out one by one the following day's bouts, displaying them to the spectators as he does so, before hand-ing them to a young referee who squats be-hind him. These are hand-written in a spe-cial form of script cal-led *sumo-ji*.

RIKISHI IN ACTION

RING AND RULES

The newly completed *dohyo* (ring) is ready for the *dohyo matsuri* (purification) the day before the beginning of the tournament. Although the tournament has not yet begun, cracks are already appearing on the dohyo surface due to the air-conditioning, which causes excessive dryness.

The *dohyo*, or ring, is the heart of sumo. What happens within the 14 foot 10 inch circle determines the fate of every professional sumo wrestler in Japan and everything that happens outside it is either preparation for the fighting on the dohyo or subsidiary to it. Indeed, it is the hard-packed clay ring circumscribed by half-buried straw bales of earth that sets sumo apart from every other kind of wrestling the world over, including the early forms of sumo that existed before the dohyo was developed some time during the latter half of the 17th century.

The ring rises about two feet above the floor at the Kokugikan and is placed on an 18-foot-square mound of hard-packed clay. As it has a central location in the arena the dohyo's size is deceptive; to the wrestlers on the dohyo the size of the circle is very small. A *rikishi* (sumo wrestler) making his *tachi-ai*, or initial charge, has only about four feet in which to manoeuvre to his rear or to one side or the other.

Sumo rules may appear complex to the uninitiated but actually they are very simple. A wrestler wins by pushing his opponent out of the circle or when any part of his opponent's body touches the clay or goes out of the ring (with the exception of the soles of his feet). Sumo has 70 basic techniques and only a few prohibitions. If a rikishi pulls the hair of his opponent, he automatically loses the bout. Punching, grabbing an opponent's belt in the *mae-bukuro* section covering the vital organs, choking and clasping one's hands behind an opponent's back are all specifically prohibited in the rules of sumo, primarily to avoid injuries.

As the wrestler's mawashi or belt is generally at least 30 feet long, the chance of this falling off are remote. Furthermore, the referee is charged with tightening belts that are too loose or come untied. However, there have been two or three instances within the last century where a rikishi has been left standing naked in the middle of a bout (the last instance being in 1946); this embarrassment can sometimes be forestalled if the wrestler has taken the precaution of wearing a *fundoshi*, or loin cloth, under the belt.

11

Below Ryogoku (left) is about to force Fujinoshin out of the ring yorikiri. In order to counter Ryogoku's tactics, and possibly throw him, Fujinoshin needs to get his left hand on Ryogoku's mawashi in an overarm grip, but just can't make it.

Right During *jungyo* (provincial tours) wrestlers don't bother to go back to the dressing room to change after the ceremonial *dohyo-iri*, as they do during tournaments. Here a juryo wrestler is being helped with his mawashi by his attendant, watched by the odd, interested spectator.

The only trouble is that not all rikishi wear fundoshi. Sumo Association rules stipulate that a wrestler automatically loses if his belt falls off.

The Sumo Association's rules mandate that rikishi in the two top divisions of Makunouchi and Juryo use tournament mawashi that are black, purple, navy blue or a similarly sober colour but many rikishi in the past 20 years have ignored this unenforced rule and sport mawashi in bright shades of orange, blue and green. The introduction of colour television undoubtedly encouraged more and more rikishi to wear brightly coloured belts. However, in the past few years the conservative colours outlined in the rules have come back into vogue.

Accidental disqualification resulting from a rikishi inadvertently pulling his opponent's hair is seen once every year or so. In some cases these 'fouls' seem to be deliberate; but it is usually because he grabs his opponent's hair in the heat of battle, not quite realizing what he has done until the referee declares his opponent the winner at the end of the bout.

Onokuni (left) has a throat grip on Takami-sugi. This is mainly used to get an opponent off balance, whereupon it is effectively followed up by another technique.

RANKINGS AND DIVISIONS

Grand Champion Chiyonofuji, in the *shikiri* position during the preliminaries of a bout. He is the oldest wrestler in the top division, which is very rare for a Grand Champion, and has already won the Emperor's Cup 27 times. Although small for the top division, his speed, power and (in particular) concentration are more than a match for any other wrestler. He is fond of golf and fishing.

Sumo is a meritocratic society with a strictly vertical hierarchy. Whereas in Japanese business and politics the hierarchy is generally determined by age and seniority, the pecking order of the rikishi is determined solely by their prowess in the ring, in other words, by their strength, size and the efforts they make. A rikishi's rank determines not only which opponents he faces and how much he earns but also his attire, his duties if any in his stable, when he eats, and to a large extent his fate after he retires from active competition. Without the *banzuke*, or ranking list, professional sumo could not exist.

A new banzuke appears on a Monday 13 days before each tournament opens. After the Sumo Association releases the new banzuke at 6.00am, the junior rikishi carry them back to their stables from the Kokugikan or, in the case of Osaka, Nagoya and Fukuoka, from the site of the tournament. The Sumo Association has about 200,000 banzuke printed, most of which are distributed among the stables. There is no training on the day the banzuke appears as the whole day is spent folding and mailing the ranking list to friends, relatives and patrons. Every man in sumo receives his allotment of ban-zuke, ranging from hundreds of copies for an established wrestler to only a few for a new recruit.

The banzuke is written in a traditional brushstroke form of *kanji* (Chinese characters) that is unique to the sumo world. All of the active wrestlers, the elders and the referees are listed. The names of the rikishi in the two top divisions are easy enough to read but discerning the ranks in the lowest divisions at the bottom of the banzuke often requires a magnifying glass, as the kanji at that level are extremely small and compressed. The ranks for the active rikishi are as follows:

Mae-Zumo: This is a qualifying class for new recruits. After passing through mae-zumo, they are then ranked in the bottom Jonokuchi division in the following tournament. In practice, all wrestlers who appear in mae-zumo-level bouts automati-

CHIYONOFUJI

Ranking **Yokozuna**
Real name **Mitsugu Akimoto**
Stable **Kokonoe**
Birthplace **Hokkaido**
Age **33**
Height **6ft 0in (183cm)**
Weight **276lb (125kg)**
Makunouchi entry **September 1975**

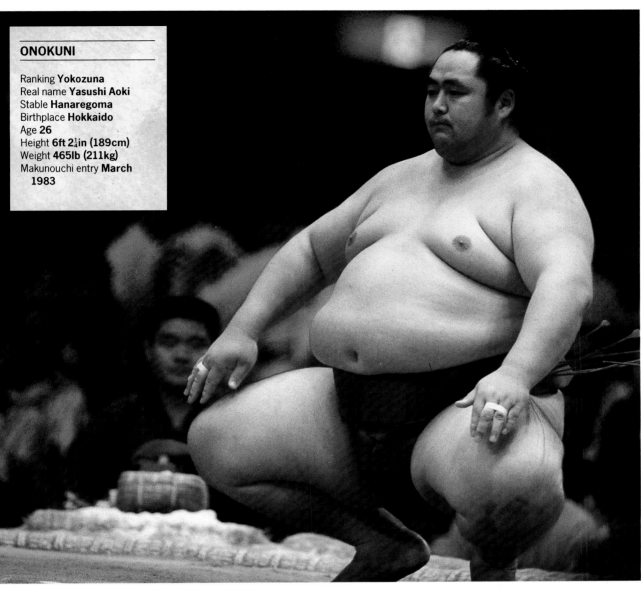

ONOKUNI

Ranking **Yokozuna**
Real name **Yasushi Aoki**
Stable **Hanaregoma**
Birthplace **Hokkaido**
Age **26**
Height **6ft 2½in (189cm)**
Weight **465lb (211kg)**
Makunouchi entry **March 1983**

Grand Champion Ono-kuni, in the *sonkyo* position of respect. Onokuni is affectionately known as the Panda. His slow gait and enormous girth belie his great strength. His weakness is his timidity, hence his nickname, but at only 26 he still has time to make a name for himself.

Below A copy of the *banzuke* is displayed during the tournament on a board in front of the stadium. It is an exact replica of the printed ones, shown (**below left**) in stacks, being collected before being folded and sent out to supporters. On the board below the banzuke is the list of bouts for that day.

15

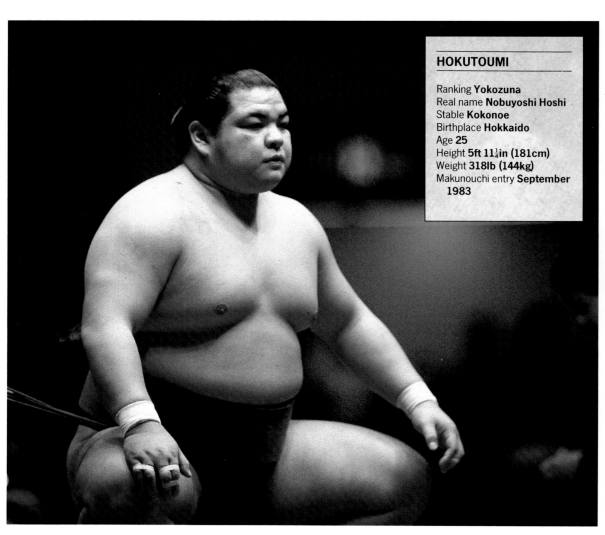

HOKUTOUMI

Ranking **Yokozuna**
Real name **Nobuyoshi Hoshi**
Stable **Kokonoe**
Birthplace **Hokkaido**
Age **25**
Height **5ft 11¼in (181cm)**
Weight **318lb (144kg)**
Makunouchi entry **September 1983**

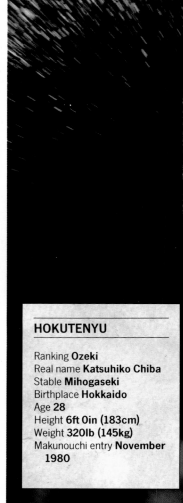

HOKUTENYU

Ranking **Ozeki**
Real name **Katsuhiko Chiba**
Stable **Mihogaseki**
Birthplace **Hokkaido**
Age **28**
Height **6ft 0in (183cm)**
Weight **320lb (145kg)**
Makunouchi entry **November 1980**

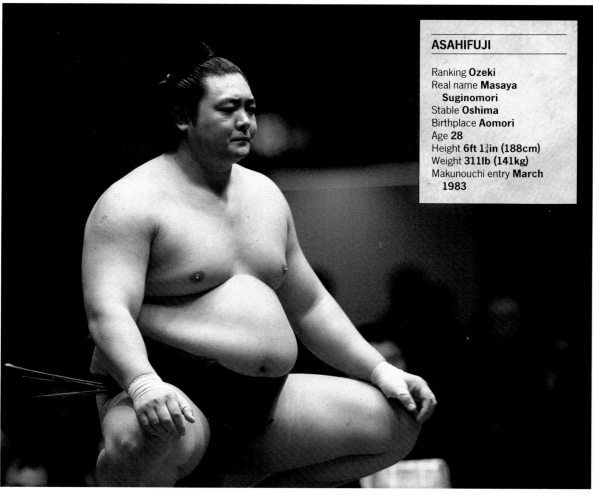

ASAHIFUJI

Ranking **Ozeki**
Real name **Masaya Suginomori**
Stable **Oshima**
Birthplace **Aomori**
Age **28**
Height **6ft 1¾in (188cm)**
Weight **311lb (141kg)**
Makunouchi entry **March 1983**

KONISHIKI

Ranking **Ozeki**
Real name **Salevaa Atisanoe**
Stable **Takasago**
Birthplace **Hawaii**
Age **25**
Height **6ft 1½in (187cm)**
Weight **503lb (228kg)**
Makunouchi entry **July 1984**

cally advance to Jonokuchi in the next tournament but rikishi who are absent in Jonokuchi fall back to mae-zumo.

Jonokuchi: This is the lowest division in sumo. There are usually about 35 ranks on both the east (*higashi*) and west (*nishi*) sides, although the division expands dramatically each May when new recruits from junior high school who finished their compulsory schooling in March are first ranked. Sometimes even a two-win, five-loss record will suffice for promotion from this division. Demotion back to the mae-zumo level – off the banzuke, in other words – generally occurs only if a rikishi has failed to participate in a tournment in this division. Achieving a perfect 7–0 record in the Jonokuchi, Jonidan and Sandanme divisions results in automatic promotion to the next division in the following tournament, however lowly ranked the division champion may have been.

Jonidan: This is sumo's largest division, generally with at least 130 ranks on each of the east and west sides. In July when new recruits advance through Jonokuchi, the Jonidan division usually expands to accommodate more than 150 or 160 ranks on each side. Even though the preliminary rituals before each bout are very brief at this level, the Jonidan bouts take up at least two hours on most days of each tournament. The average age of rikishi in this division is between 16 and 19.

Sandanme: There are 100 ranks on both the east and west sides in the Sandanme division. Fewer than half of all wrestlers progress beyond Jonidan and, for many of those that do, Sandanme is a barrier beyond which they are unable to advance. Most of the wrestlers in this division

Far left Grand Champion Hokutoumi. He came back in Osaka to win the Emperor's Cup after an absence from three tournaments due to a back injury. He has already won four tournaments, and could still fight for a long time and win many more.

Left Champion Hokutenyu, in his early days in the top ranks was, and probably still is, one of the strongest wrestlers in maku-nouchi and could still make yokozuna given the will. He already has two tournament wins to his credit. Win or lose he always appears the coolest wrestler on or off the dohyo.

Far left Ozeki Asahifuji would probably have been made yokozuna by now but in a tournament in Osaka Chiyono-fuji had to default through injury and Asahifuji was denied the chance of beating him and gaining promotion to yokozuna. His suppleness and the difficulty the others have of grabbing hold of him have given him the nickname of Sea-slug.

Left Konishiki is the top foreigner (non-Japanese) in sumo and the only one ever to have been made Champion. His real name is Salevaa Atisanoe and he comes from Hawaii. His weight and the strain it puts on an injured right knee caused him to lose badly a few times, but he has managed to lose weight and is looking much stronger and more agile.

Far right Sakahoko, the second of three sumo brothers, has a 20th-century record of being sekiwake for nine consecutive tournaments. Although since demoted to komusubi, he could easily make it back to sekiwake again. He has the ability to beat yokozuna and ozeki but does not seem to have the consistency or determination to become ozeki himself, even though he is still not too old.

are in their late teens or early 20s, though there are a few veterans in their late 20s or early 30s.

Makushita: Makushita may be translated as 'below the curtain'. Most of the rikishi who advance to this division never rise above the curtain. Competition is fierce and some of the best sumo bouts are at this level. There are always 60 ranks on each side of the division, with an auxiliary rank added when a college champion makes his professional debut. Makushita competitors range

in age from late teens to mid-30s and include many rikishi demoted from the top division. From time to time a declining former sekiwake will drop this low. Tochiakagi, for instance, was ranked as Makushita 14 east in March 1989, eight years after he fought as a sekiwake (third highest rank in the top division) in September 1980. A rikishi will automatically be promoted to Juryo if he has a perfect 7–0 record in the top 15 ranks on either side of this division. Former college champions, including Wajima, Asashio, Kushima

and in January 1989 Yamazaki, made their debut at the bottom of Makushita instead of starting from scratch at mae-zumo.

Juryo: Rikishi at this level were once paid 10 *ryo* (the currency of the late Edo Period). What is now Juryo was once the top 10 ranks of Makushita, and it was only in 1889 that Juryo was made a separate division from Makushita. The difference in status between Juryo and Makushita is striking – Juryo are fully-fledged fighters with their own colourful

Right Terao's main complaint is that he is too light and finds it difficult to put on weight. His promotion to the rank of sekiwake in March 1989 (when he and Sakahoko became the first brothers to have held the rank at the same time) is proof of his endeavour. He is one of the most popular wrestlers among all kinds of fans. He has beaten Konishiki on a few occasions. His main technique is *tsuppari* (thrusting) and in 30 seconds he has been recorded as landing between 50 to a 100 blows to his opponent's face and chest.

Far right Kotogaume is a pusher and thruster. He has been consistent enough to stay in or near sanyaku for years. With a very low centre of gravity, he is a formidable adversary, and moves like a small tank. Yet he is amazingly good natured and considerate.

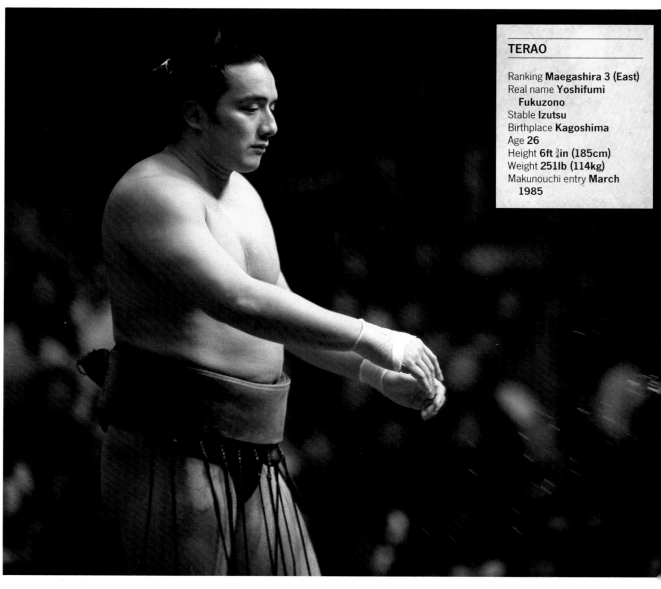

TERAO

Ranking **Maegashira 3 (East)**
Real name **Yoshifumi Fukuzono**
Stable **Izutsu**
Birthplace **Kagoshima**
Age **26**
Height **6ft ¾in (185cm)**
Weight **251lb (114kg)**
Makunouchi entry **March 1985**

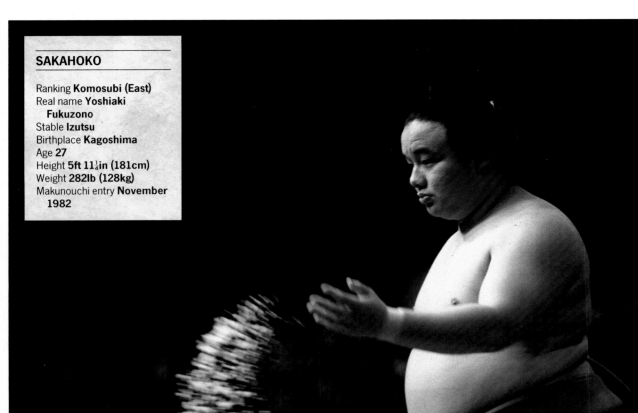

SAKAHOKO

Ranking **Komosubi (East)**
Real name **Yoshiaki Fukuzono**
Stable **Izutsu**
Birthplace **Kagoshima**
Age **27**
Height **5ft 11¼in (181cm)**
Weight **282lb (128kg)**
Makunouchi entry **November 1982**

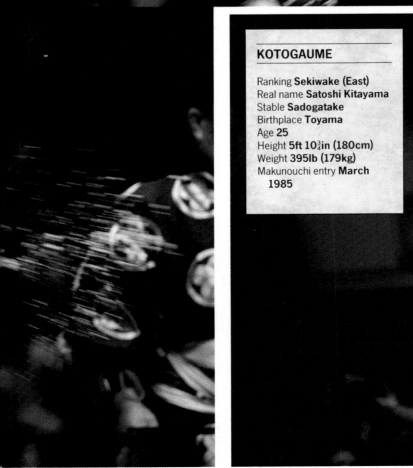

KOTOGAUME

Ranking **Sekiwake (East)**
Real name **Satoshi Kitayama**
Stable **Sadogatake**
Birthplace **Toyama**
Age **25**
Height **5ft 10¾in (180cm)**
Weight **395lb (179kg)**
Makunouchi entry **March 1985**

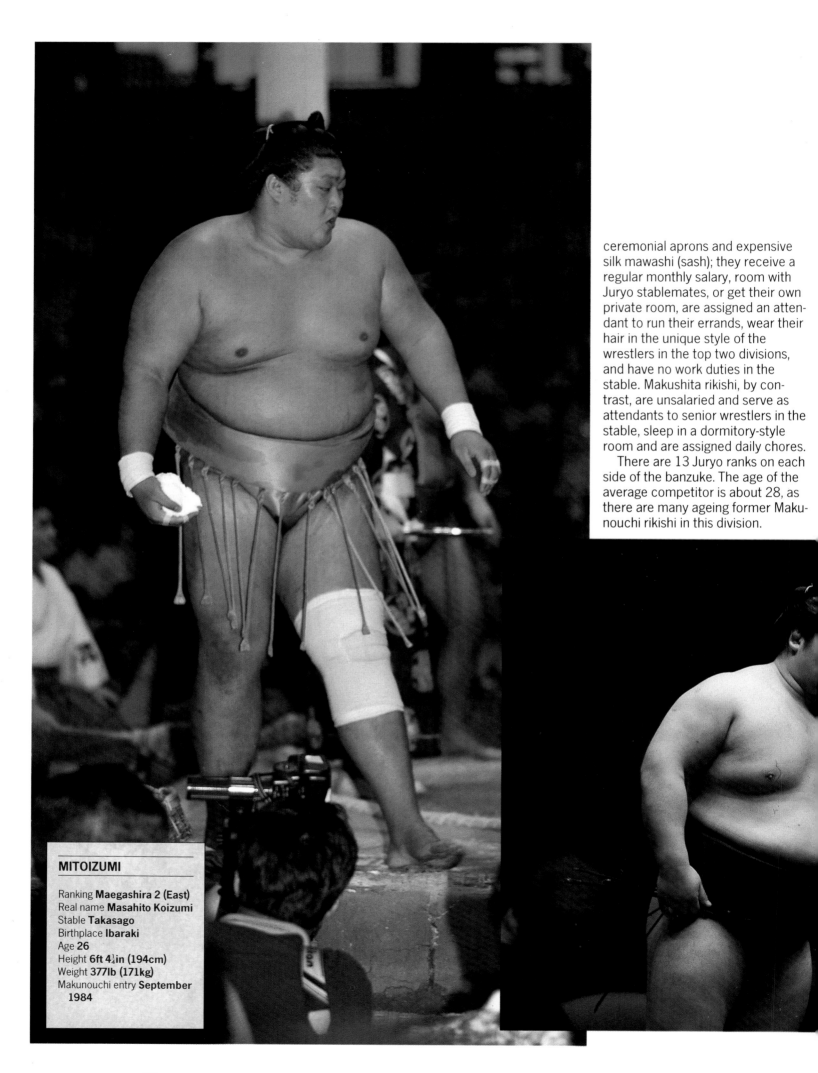

ceremonial aprons and expensive silk mawashi (sash); they receive a regular monthly salary, room with Juryo stablemates, or get their own private room, are assigned an attendant to run their errands, wear their hair in the unique style of the wrestlers in the top two divisions, and have no work duties in the stable. Makushita rikishi, by contrast, are unsalaried and serve as attendants to senior wrestlers in the stable, sleep in a dormitory-style room and are assigned daily chores.

There are 13 Juryo ranks on each side of the banzuke. The age of the average competitor is about 28, as there are many ageing former Makunouchi rikishi in this division.

MITOIZUMI

Ranking **Maegashira 2 (East)**
Real name **Masahito Koizumi**
Stable **Takasago**
Birthplace **Ibaraki**
Age **26**
Height **6ft 4¼in (194cm)**
Weight **377lb (171kg)**
Makunouchi entry **September 1984**

Far left Mitoizumi's nickname is the Salt Shaker because of the amount of salt he uses for his final throw. Previously he used to throw that much salt every time but was told by the Sumo Association to cut it out. In 1985 he was already sanyaku when he was involved in a traffic accident that put him out for some tourna- ments. Then he hurt his knee and was sidelined again for a while. With another good record he could be back in sanyaku again shortly and still has plenty of time to make ozeki. In his spare time likes reading.

Below Kyokudozan comes from the same heya as Asahifuji – in fact the 'Kyoku' in his name is another read- ing of the Chinese char- acter 'Asahi'. Kyokudo- zan is considered to be one of the most prom- ising of the rikishi now in makunouchi, so much so that Chiyonofuji singled him out for practice and said that he considers Kyokudo- zan a younger version of himself. At only 100kg (about 218lbs) he is the lightest rikishi in makunouchi and should do well once he gains weight and ex- perience.

Makunouchi: The top division of sumo. Literally, it means 'inside the curtain'. It is sub-divided into the following ranks:

Maegashira: Maegashira are the lower-ranked rikishi in the top division. There are generally 13 or 14 maegashira on each side of the banzuke.

Komusubi: This is the first of the sanyaku rankings which culminate with the yokozuna. These days most rikishi who reach Makunouchi go as far as komusubi at least once. Of current fighters, Takanofuji and Sasshunada, however, are two of the veterans in Makunouchi who have yet to reach komusubi after several years in the top division. Promotion

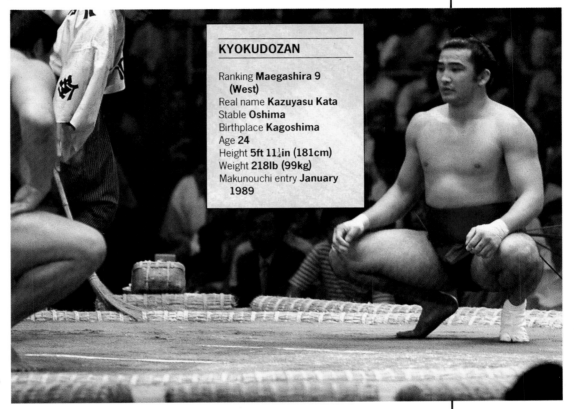

KYOKUDOZAN

Ranking **Maegashira 9 (West)**
Real name **Kazuyasu Kata**
Stable **Oshima**
Birthplace **Kagoshima**
Age **24**
Height **5ft 11¼in (181cm)**
Weight **218lb (99kg)**
Makunouchi entry **January 1989**

AKINOSHIMA

Ranking **Sekiwake (West)**
Real name **Katsumi Yamanaka**
Stable **Fujishima**
Birthplace **Hiroshima**
Age **23**
Height **5ft 9in (176cm)**
Weight **293lb (132kg)**
Makunouchi entry **March 1988**

to sekiwake may be possible from this rank with an 8–7 record; but some rikishi have been held at komusubi with a 10–5 score be- cause there were no vacancies in sekiwake – the Sumo Kyokai resists ranking more than two rikishi at komusubi or sekiwake.

Sekiwake: Sekiwake is a crucial rank and the first stepping-stone upward in the quest for promotion to ozeki. A 7–8 record at sekiwake will usually result in demotion to komusubi and anything less than that brings almost certain demotion to the maegashira ranks. A wrestler is expected to win at least 30 bouts in three consecutive tournaments at sekiwake to qualify for promotion, though there have been exceptions. In the 1989 March Tournament, Sakahoko set a new all-time record for being ranked as sekiwake for nine consecutive basho. In the same tournament his younger brother Terao reached sekiwake for the first

time since gaining promotion to Makunouchi four years earlier.

Ozeki: Literally, this means the 'great barrier'. Less than half of the wrestlers who reach this far event- ually attain yokozuna promotion, while only one in 300 new sumo wrestlers reaches ozeki. Promotion to yokozuna is achieved through two consecutive tournament wins or almost equivalent records, including runner-up honours. Demotion is automatic after two straight losing records.

Yokozuna: This is the ultimate rank in sumo, and one from which there is no further promotion – or demotion. Before 1890, yokozuna was only an honorary status given to outstanding ozeki. In more than 250 years of professional sumo there have been only 62 yokozuna. Although yokozuna cannot be de- moted, they will be encouraged to retire if they have continuously poor records.

Left Akinoshima is one of the most promising young wrestlers in the top division. It took him only eight tournaments in makunouchi to make sanyaku rank, and he has already been awarded three of the sansho, one for out- standing performance and two for fighting spirit. He is said to have set himself a mark of at least 100 practice bouts a day.

RITUALS AND RELIGION

立入禁止

一般の方は
入れませ/

Three of the top gyoji – tate-gyoji Shikimori Inosuke flanked by Shikimori Taichiro (left) and Shikimori Kindayu – waiting in the aisle to go on for the dohyo matsuri, the ceremony of purification that is always carried out on the Saturday before a tournament.

Sumo's roots and rituals are almost all derived from Shinto, the indigenous religion of Japan. While there have been some modifications in the basic sumo rituals, most have remained unchanged since the Edo Period (1616–1867).

On the day before each tournament starts, a Shinto ceremony is held to purify the newly rebuilt ring (dohyo). Called the dohyo matsuri, it is also performed to pray for the safety of the rikishi who will compete over the following two weeks. The ceremony is conducted by the chief referee, Kimura Shonosuke, or by the next-highest-ranked gyoji, Shikimore Inosuke, who acts as a Shinto priest during the purification rituals.

The dohyo-iri, the ring-entering ceremony of the Makunouchi and Juryo divisions as well as of the yokozuna, is an ancient sumo ritual designed to show that the competitors carry no concealed weapons. There are two forms of the yokozuna dohyo-iri: Unryu-gata and Shiranui-gata. The Unryu-gata is said to have originated with yokozuna Unryu (1823–91) but it has recently been attributed instead to yokozuna Shiranui Koemon (1825–79). The so-called Shiranui-gata dohyo-iri was actually first performed in its present form by yokozuna Tachiyama in 1911. The two styles of yokozuna dohyo-iri are very similar, the only significant difference being that in the Unryu-gata ceremony the yoko-

zuna rises with both arms outstretched. The tsuna, or white hawser, of the Unryu-gata yokozuna is tied together with a single loop at the back, while the Shiranui-gata hawser has two loops. There have been only seven Shiranui-gata yokozuna and most of them had very short tenures at sumo's highest rank or have suffered some other misfortune.

A yokozuna usually performs his final dohyo-iri at his intai-zumo (retirement) ceremony. However, if he lives to be 60 and is still in sufficiently good health, he performs the dohyo-iri in a red tsuna to celebrate his birthday with a ceremony called kanreki dohyo-iri. Kanreki, the completion of five 12-year cycles of the

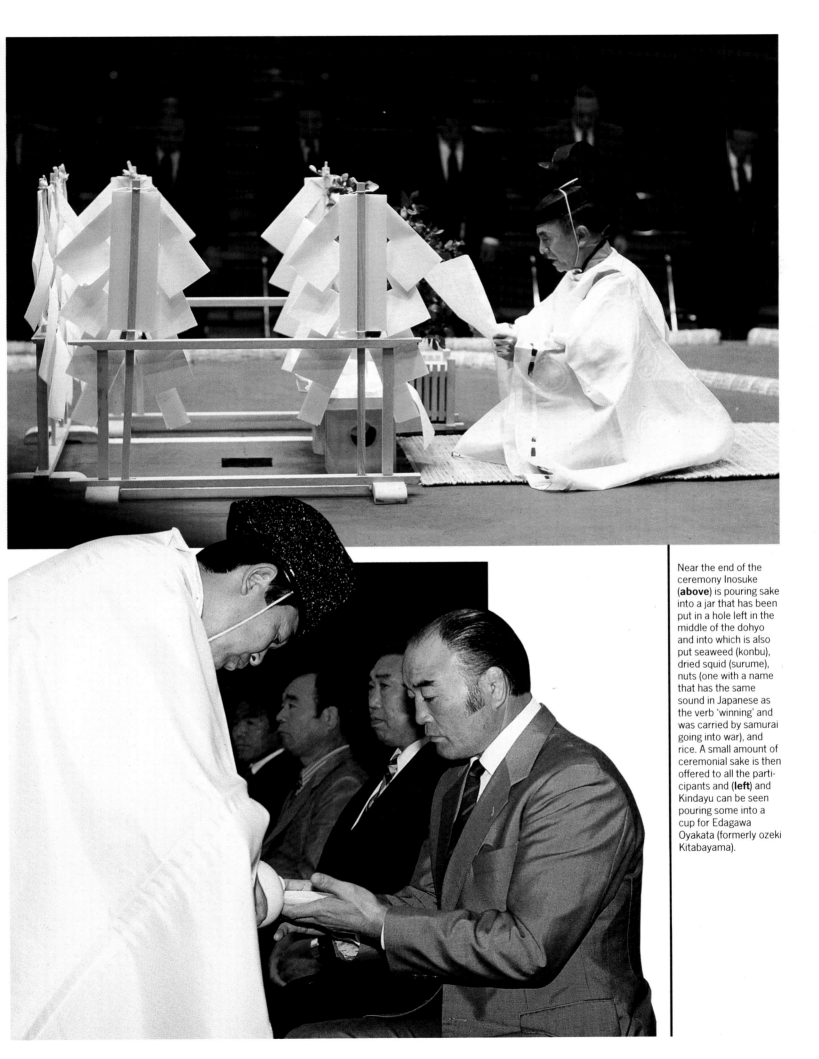

Near the end of the ceremony Inosuke (**above**) is pouring sake into a jar that has been put in a hole left in the middle of the dohyo and into which is also put seaweed (konbu), dried squid (surume), nuts (one with a name that has the same sound in Japanese as the verb 'winning' and was carried by samurai going into war), and rice. A small amount of ceremonial sake is then offered to all the participants and (**left**) and Kindayu can be seen pouring some into a cup for Edagawa Oyakata (formerly ozeki Kitabayama).

23

Above As with a day of sumo itself, everything begins and ends with the drumming of the yobidashi. Masahiro and Norio can be seen doing the honours walking around the dohyo at the end of a dohyo matsuri.

zodiac, is considered to be an auspicious occasion for any man or woman in Japan, Korea and China. Only five yokozuna have performed their kanreki dohyo-iri, the most recent being Tochinishiki in 1985 and Wakanohana I in 1988. The Japanese now enjoy the longest average lifespan in the world and rikishi are also living much longer than they did 20 or 30 years ago, so the kanreki dohyo-iri will undoubtedly become more common.

The *shussei-hiro* ceremony introduces to the fans the new recruits who have passed the mae-zumo qualification round. The boys borrow *kesho-mawashi* aprons from the sekitori or *oyakata* (elders) in their own or a related stable for this ceremony, in which their name, home prefecture and stable are announced, after which they bow and leave the ring.

The *sanyaku soroibumi* takes place only on the final day of an official tournament. The last three wrestlers on each side enter the dohyo, clap their hands and then stamp their feet twice. The sanyaku soroibumi is also performed at one-day *hana-zumo* tourneys.

There are several rituals connected with the bout itself (see the next section on 'Bouts').

Besides the various sumo ceremonies that don't take place during tournaments, the yokozuna dohyo-iri is regularly performed at Meiji Jingu and other important Shinto shrines. A ritual of sorts has been developed for the *danpatsu-shiki*, or hair-cutting ceremony, of a retiring wrestler. The rikishi sits in formal kimono on the dohyo, with his supporters preceding the stablemaster in making the final cut on his topknot.

Sandan-gamae is one of the least-frequently-seen rituals. It is not performed during an official tournament and is only staged on special occasions, the most recent being the opening ceremony of the new

During the day the most colourful ceremonies or rituals are the *dohyo-iri*, performed by the jury rikishi immediately before their bouts begin, at about two-fifty, and then the *makunouchi* and yokozuna dohyo-iri at about four o'clock. The rikishi file on anti-clockwise, with those ranked lowest leading the field, and first they face outwards. This is part of the makunouchi dohyo-iri with (left to right) Akinoshima, Takamisugi and Kotoinazuma, and behind them in the centre, gyoji Kimura Rinnosuke.

Above After the makunouchi dohyo-iri come those of the yokozuna, led by a tate-gyoji (out of the picture), a dew-sweeper (Fujinoshin), and followed by a sword-bearer (Takanofuji). The yokozuna, in this case Chiyonofuji, first performs the *chiri-chozu* ceremony, showing that he has no concealed weapons.

Kokugikan in January 1985. In the sandan-gamae, two yokozuna – or one yokozuna and one ozeki or, very rarely, two ozeki – display their strength by stretching out one of their arms toward each other from an upper, middle and lower position. A referee squats slightly behind their extended fingertips, holding his *gunbai* (war fan) flat and extended outward at forehead level.

All daily sumo performances, both official basho and hana-zumo tournaments, end with the *yumitori-shiki*, a 400-year-old bow-twirling ceremony in which a Makushita or Sandanme rikishi represents the final winner of the day in accepting the thanks of the wrestlers for the spectators present.

Like most Japanese, sumo wrestlers hold no special religious loyalty. Their weddings are usually held as Shinto ceremonies, whereas their funerals are generally held as Buddhist ceremonies.

Far right The *seriagari*. Where possible tsuyu-harai and tachi-mochi come from the same heya as the yokozuna, as in the case of Fujinoshin and Takanofuji, or from the same *ichimon*, or group of related heya. They must be makunouchi rikishi.

Right On the final day of a tournament, the sanyaku, or top three rikishi on either side, perform a ceremony called the sanyaku *soroi-bumi* (line-up of the sanyaku). Konishiki, Asahifuji and Chiyonofuji are performing the ceremony.

26

BOUTS

A rikishi's success or failure in sumo depends entirely on how he performs in the ring. If he wins more bouts than he loses, he rises in the sumo world; if he suffers more defeats than wins, he slips down the ranks. But it is his consistency over a tournament that counts.

A sumo bout includes everything that happens from the time the two wrestlers climb into the ring after their names have been called out until the winner receives his bout-prize envelope (Makunouchi bouts only) and steps back off the dohyo. In the top division the average bout lasts about 30 seconds, although some may occasionally take as long as six or seven minutes or more. After mounting the dohyo the rikishi perform the *chiri-chozu* ceremony at opposite edges of the dohyo. The two wrestlers squat on their haunches, extend their arms outward, clap their hands once, extend their arms again and turn the palms of their hands upward and then down. Next, they go to the centre of the ring and do *shiko* – lifting one leg sideways high in the air and stamping it down hard on the dohyo.

The two opponents then go to their respective sides of the dohyo, receive a dipper of power-water and rinse out their mouth, which they wipe with a paper towel. On one side, the water and paper are handed up by the winner of the previous bout, but on the other side this is done by the wrestler waiting to fight in the following bout. Since the winner symbolically passes on his power to the next wrestler, the loser of the previous bout never does it, but leaves right after the bout is over; the only exception to this is that the loser in the penultimate match waits at ringside until the final bout is over.

The two rikishi then dip their hand into a basket of unrefined salt set up in the corner, turn and scatter the salt on the dohyo as they stride towards the centre of the ring. They stop on reaching two white lines that mark the starting point for each wrestler, crouch down on their haunches and lean forward on their fists, glaring at each other, eyeball to eyeball. The salt-tossing, or *shikiri*, is often a trademark of particular fighters, with some like Mitoizumi showering the dohyo with a huge handful of salt just after *jikan-ippai* (time is up) is indicated and others like the huge Konishiki throwing out only a tiny bit of salt pinched delicately between two fingers.

This ritual is repeated six or seven times until the timekeeper signals by raising his right hand that it's time to start fighting. In the old days, there was no time limit for the shikiri,

Asahifuji and Chiyono-fuji sit on either side of Kimigahama Shimpan (ex-sekiwake Kitase-umi) awaiting their turn (with Konishiki along for the sanyaku soroi-bumi). They are already keyed up and each shows his character, either feigning indifference or showing complete confidence, like Chiyonofuji, scowling like Hokutomi or Masurao, or staring their opponent down, as some wrestlers do.

Right When their name is called the wrestlers climb onto the dohyo and then go to the their corner, where they first stamp the devils into the ground. Looking at Konishiki from behind, one could sympathise with a devil underneath his feet.

Right After stamping the devils, the wrestler crouches down and receives 'power-water' from the previous rikishi (as Chiyonofuji is doing from Hokutomi), who stays behind for this purpose if he has won, or from the next rikishi on that side to fight, if the previous rikishi has lost.

The rikishi grabs some salt which he throws onto the dohyo and advances to the centre. Salt is used in Shinto to purify, but in sumo also acts as a cleansing agent for rikishi who may graze or cut themselves.

especially for the top bouts. There is a story about how a sumo fan was hurriedly called away on business at the beginning of the final bout between two yokozuna; when he returned to his seat more than half an hour later, the two grand champions were still going through the shikiri ritual. Because the top-division bouts are now televised and have to fit in with the schedules, the shikiri is limited to four minutes (three minutes in Juryo).

The salt ceremony is to purify the ring and also serves to create a good, slippery mixture with the sand for sliding the feet. Some western fans find this ritual tedious but it does help to build up tension and excitement in the audience. It also gives the spectators time to digest the result of the just-concluded match and prepare themselves for the forthcoming bout. Remember that there are over 350 bouts every day during the tournament; this seemingly endless parade of bouts one after another, many of them finished within a few brief seconds, would leave the spectator's mind in a whirl if there were no time to adjust from one bout to the next.

The first time the rikishi advances to the centre of the ring he performs the chirichozu (ceremony showing that he has no weapons concealed in his hand), as Konishiki is doing.

Far left After going back to his corner for more salt the rikishi squats down in *sonkyo* position of respect, as the two makushita rikishi.

Left The rikishi then crouches and leans forward on his side of one of the two lines (*shikiri-sen*).

Above During the repeated shikiri the wrestlers will try to psyche each other out, as Tochinowaka (left) and Itai are doing. This can have the opposite effect to that desired.

Right To accommodate TV, which shows sumo only until six o'clock, bouts are now timed. Kimigahama Oyakata, who is acting as timekeeper, is indicating to the gyoji that time for the preliminaries is up.

Some rikishi use the shikiri to engage in psychological warfare and silently try to disturb the composure of their opponent with fierce glares. The yokozuna and ozeki especially try to intimidate their lower-ranked opponents, as the fans shout out the names of their favourites and build themselves into a fever pitch of excitement, particularly in the crucial matches towards the end of the tournament. Ozeki Konishiki and Hokutenyu are notorious for their attempts to occasionally stare down their opponents. However, while he was climbing up the ranks of the top division, Chiyonofuji was probably the staring champion. When he was a young rikishi, he was given the nickname of 'the Wolf' by his stablemaster, Kokonoe Oyakata (ex-yokozuna Kitanofuji), because of his wild eyes and sharp features.

One of the five judges sitting around the ring doubles as timekeeper and raises his hand to indicate that the two wrestlers must start fighting the next time they come to the centre of the ring. To warn them that the shikiri is over, the attendants stand up in their respective corners and hand the combatants a towel to use in wiping the sweat off their body. As the two rikishi brace themselves for the *tachi-ai*, or opening charge, the referee raises his war-fan from a horizontal to a vertical position. This is like the starter's gun at the beginning of a race. This is the moment of truth for sumo wrestlers, the instant when most bouts are either won or lost. It is said that the tachi-ai is 70 per cent of a bout. A hard-charging wrestler may boom his opponent out of the ring with the momentum gained from this initial collision or an agile rikishi may sidestep his rampaging foe and pull him ingloriously down on to all fours.

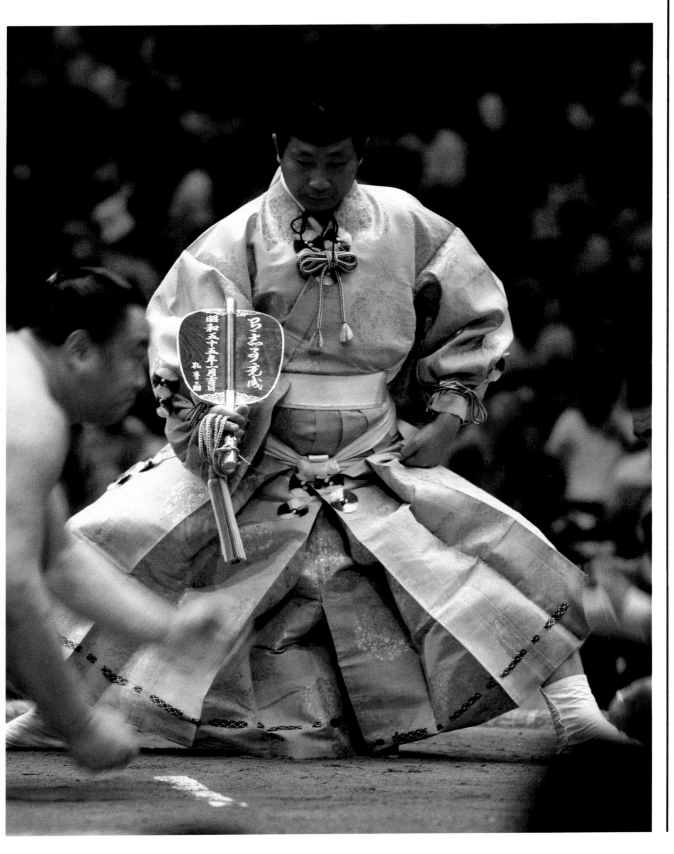

Kimura Koichi has told the rikishi to start and turned his war fan (*gumbai*) back in the starting pose known as 'jikan no kata'.

Far right The *tachiai* is so similar to the shikiri that rikishi have been known to start fighting before the gyoji has told them it is time to do so. Often the result is a head-on collision and it usually decides the outcome.

In the final stages of the shikiri the wrestlers attune themselves to one another, so that they will rise from their haunches simultaneously to launch their opening charge. If one is not ready, he doesn't have to accept the start of the bout when his opponent charges across at him, calling *'Matta!'* ('Not yet!').

Occasionally, a rikishi indulges in a little gamesmanship by making a deliberate false start to get his opponent off his timing. In most cases, though, saying matta is simply due to nervousness on the part of one or both rikishi, who have not quite reached a state of mental and physical readiness. In one bout in the 1970s the two wrestlers made seven false starts before the bout got started.

The referee must immediately point his fan towards the rikishi he deems to be the winner no matter how close the outcome. If any of the five judges disputes the referee's decision, he will raise his hand and call for a *mono-ii*, a judges' conference. In a rare concession to modern technology, the chief judge is connected by a direct wire and earplug to another official in a separate room monitoring the bouts on video slow-motion playback and will take this official's report into consideration during the mono-ii. The judges then have three alternatives: to call for a rematch, to announce a confirmation of the referee's original decision or to overturn the referee's decision.

Too many wrong decisions can result in the referee's demotion or being passed over for promotion in the future. The chief referee, Kimura Shonosuke, who officiates at only the final bout each day, must immediately submit his resignation if his decision is overturned, although it is only a formality and is almost never accepted. He is not expected to participate in the judges' conference at mid-ring unless he is invited to do so.

Right One rikishi sometimes jumps the gun and moves before the other one is ready. The other one will then call 'Matta!' ('Not yet!'), as Masudayama has done.

Centre right Shimpan Magaki Oyakata (former yokozuna Wakanohana II), as the one best positioned to judge, is raising his hand to show that one rikishi has put his foot out and lost. The gyoji officiating will simultaneously declare that the bout has been won and point his war fan towards the side of the winning rikishi.

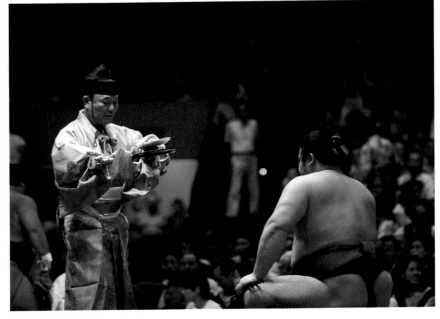

Once the bout is over the rikishi return to their respective sides; the loser will bow out and the gyoji will call the name of the winner and present him the *kensho* (sponsorship awards) on his fan, as Kimura Shotaro is doing.

TECHNIQUES

Many bouts begin with a kind of pushing/ slapping called *tsup-pari*, which sometimes can overwhelm an opponent so that he is pushed back out of the dohyo, the object of both rikishi below.

Although there are 70 official techniques, less than a third of them are used in the average tournament in the top division and today some are almost never seen. Although sumo techniques were known as *shiju hatte*, or 48 techniques, the Sumo Kyokai officially recognized the use of 70 sumo techniques in 1960.

Simplified, most wrestlers fall roughly into the two basic types: *oshi-zumo* (pushing) and *yotsu-zumo* (belt fighting). Thus the two most commonly used techniques are *oshidashi* (the push-out) and *yorikiri* (the frontal force-out). But thrusting and arm-throwing attacks are used almost as frequently and the most common winning variations of these tactics are thrust-out and overarm-throw. Other popular tactics include the outside leg trip, slapping off-balance, twisting down to one side or the other, hoisting out of the ring, pulling forward off-balance and driving over backwards such as the backward force-down.

Besides the 70 official techniques, there are two other ways of winning or rather losing a bout. One is by stepping out of the ring by mistake just when it seems the rikishi is about to win. The other way of losing

The most common technique involves pushing a rikishi out, as Konishiki is doing to Sadanoumi here.

Terao is famous for the tsuppari technique of pushing/slapping, and is seen (left) using it against Daijuyama.

A device for breaking another rikishi's hold is the double arm-lock called *kinedashi*, which Takanofuji (left) has on Jingaku.

occurs when a wrestler's hips suddenly collapse and he inadvertently falls to the clay without being helped by his opponent.

In the early days of professional sumo, some of the leading wrestlers developed their own techniques that were added to the list of officially sanctioned techniques; these days, however, no new techniques are forthcoming. Nevertheless, certain

Right The stronger rikishi usually prefer fighting on the belt, or *mawashi*, as do Chiyonofuji and Hokutenyu.

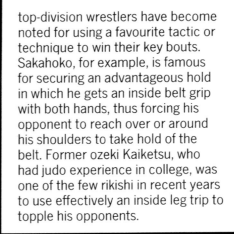

The *yori-kori* or force-out technique is used here by Hokutoumi on Hananokuni.

top-division wrestlers have become noted for using a favourite tactic or technique to win their key bouts. Sakahoko, for example, is famous for securing an advantageous hold in which he gets an inside belt grip with both hands, thus forcing his opponent to reach over or around his shoulders to take hold of the belt. Former ozeki Kaiketsu, who had judo experience in college, was one of the few rikishi in recent years to use effectively an inside leg trip to topple his opponents.

Below The *inashi*, a kind of brush-off, is tried by Jingaku (right) on Takanofuji.

Right A kinedashi that one of the heaviest rikishi in the game, a makushita rikishi named Maeda (left), has on another rikishi of similar rank.

Right A kinedashi that one of the heaviest rikishi in the game, a makushita rikishi named Maeda (left), has on another rikishi of similar rank.

Far right A spectacular shot for a lucky photographer – but it is difficult to see quite who is doing what to whom, or who actually won!

Right A hataki-komi being performed by the expert Terao, who is beating Kinoarashi, a rikishi almost twice his weight and size.

Of the 38 rikishi in Makunouchi in the 1989 March Tournament, about 16 were *tsuki/oshi* wrestlers, relying on thrusting and pushing as the mainstay of their attack. At least six or seven of them are also skilful on the belt, able not only to hold their own in *yotsu-zumo* bouts but also to win with belt techniques. These include yokozuna Hokutoumi, and maegashira Ryogoku, Kotoinazuma, Tochinowaka, Koboyama and Taka-nohama. On the other hand, there are a few yotsu-zumo wrestlers who sometimes win with pushing or thrusting attacks such as yokozuna Onokuni, ozeki Asahifuji and maegashira Jingaku. In November 1988 for example, Asahifuji won

four of his 12 bouts by either push-out or thrust-out. Hokutoumi is one of those rare rikishi who is equally good at tsuki/oshi techniques and yotsu-zumo.

REFEREES AND OTHERS

Below Although the actions and forms that the gyoji go through are basically the same for all, the speed of the bouts in the lower ranks allows very little time for pomp, even if the gyoji were capable of it. Here a lower-ranked gyoji has taken up the position of shikiri no kata for the one shikiri allowed before the bout begins.

Gyoji

The *gyoji* are the referees of sumo. There are currently more than 40 gyoji, ranging in age from 15 to 64. They are allotted to divisions and ranked just as rikishi are but promotion is very slow. A gyoji who makes too many *sashi-chigai* (instances where his decision on the outcome of the bout has been challenged and overturned by the judges) will be passed over for promotion. Even a very able young gyoji will only be promoted up the ladder when one of the senior referees reaches the retirement age of 65, retires early or dies.

Almost all gyoji are recruited at 15 when they finish their compulsory education. Some of the new recruits had hopes of becoming wrestlers but were either too short or too light. Young gyoji are assigned to serve as attendants to gyoji with *sekitori* status (Maku-nouchi or Juryo level) and are taught the fundamentals of refereeing bouts and the finer points of *sumo-ji,*

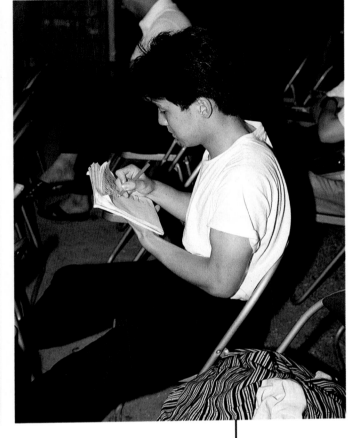

kanji characters written in a style unique to sumo. New gyoji quickly advance to the Jonokuchi, Jonidan and Sandanme divisions but from there promotion is painfully slow. The average gyoji does not attain Juryo status until he is in his late 30s and has been a referee for over 20 years. The wrestlers who made their first appearances in the same tournament that he did are all long retired. Referees officiate at bouts barefoot until they achieve Juryo status, at which time they are permitted to wear white split-toed shoe-socks. They advance to Makunouchi after about 10 years in Juryo.

The two top-ranked gyoji carry a small sword tucked under the *obi* of their kimono to symbolize the gravity of their position. The sword symbolizes suicide in the event of an incorrect judgement. No gyoji, of course, commits suicide if he mis-

judges a bout but if one of the two top referees has his decision over-turned, he will usually submit a standard resignation notice to the Sumo Association. Only once has such a 'resignation' request been accepted, however.

All gyoji take names that begin with either Kimura or Shikimori, the two symbolic families of referees. The chief referee is always named Kimura Shonosuke, while his second-in-command is always Shiki-mori Inosuke. The two top referees' names are treated by the Sumo Association as *toshiyori*, or retired names for wrestlers. The chief ref-erees thus are formally members of the Sumo Association but when they retire, they don't sell the name to their successor. The present Kimura Shonosuke, who only officiates at the final bout of the day, is over 60 and has been in the sumo world

since January 1936. He has been on the Sumo Association's payroll longer than anyone else. Most of the other referees in the upper part of the top division have also been in the sport since the pre-war era. Gyoji seem to live longer than most Japanese. In 1989, three former Kimura Shonosuke were still alive at 99, 91 and 80 years of age.

In addition to their duties on the dohyo, gyoji are assigned other tasks related to the Sumo Associa-tion and to the stable to which they belong. A senior referee has the awesome task of preparing the new ranking list. This takes two weeks and during that period he is not allowed to leave his home, as the rankings are kept confidential until the day they are officially announced. The new rankings are actually decided by the Judging Division of the Sumo Association.

43

Top yobidashi Kankichi, who entered the sumo world over 40 years ago when he was still only a boy in primary school, is here seen calling the name of the next rikishi. Some spectators think the yobidashi has names written on his fan, but the fan must be perfectly white, and young yobidashi usually carry the names of the rikishi they are calling rolled up in their left hand for reference before each bout.

Yobidashi

Yobidashi, or ring attendants, call out the names of the wrestlers appearing in each bout before they enter the dohyo, and frequently sweep the ring. New yobidashi are recruited by the sumo stables in much the same way as are new gyoji. Whereas gyoji are masters in writing the complex sumo-ji, yobidashi are taught the finer points of sumo *taiko*, or the traditional drumming at the end of a day's bouts. Yobidashi are not listed on the banzuke and don't have a formally designated ranking system. However, the most experienced yobidashi are the *de facto* leaders. Though yobidashi retire two years earlier than referees, at 63, a few have been in the sumo world since pre-war days.

Wakamono-gashira

Wakamono-gashira, a title emanating from the Edo Period, are former rikishi retained by the Sumo Kyokai to help manage the younger rikishi in the stable to which they belong. The Sumo Kyokai rules stipulate that there must be no more than eight wakamono-gashira. Until recently, they were usually former Juryo or Makushita rikishi who didn't qualify, or couldn't afford their own toshiyori name. Now, with the soaring price of toshiyori stock, one former Makunouchi rikishi, Shishiho, has become a wakamono-gashira.

Wakamono-gashira are also responsible for managing new sumo recruits and keeping an official record of their debut performance. The position is a demanding one, and a retiring rikishi hoping to become a wakamono-gashira must have the recommendation of all the *oyakata* (elders) in his stable. The retirement age for these men has in recent years been extended to 63. As most rikishi who become wakamono-gashira retire from active wrestling by the time they are 30, they are assured of their livelihood until they reach an age at which they are eligible for a government pension.

Sewanin

At one time, yobidashi, wakamono-gashira and sewanin were listed on the banzuke, but the practice was discontinued in 1959 after only 10 years. Like wakamono-gashira, sewanin are generally ex-Juryo and Makushita rikishi. However, two former maegashira have become new sewanin in the last few years. Sewanin are sent as advance men to prepare for *jungyo* exhibitions, help with ticket sales and other tasks for the Sumo Kyokai. Again, they retire at 63 and there can only be eight at one time. Though the responsibilities of the sewanin are even more closely tied to the Sumo Kyokai than are those of wakamono-gashira, they remain members of the stables to which they belonged during their active career.

In the old Osaka sumo world, a sewanin was a junior oyakata and could become a full oyakata when he had raised the money to buy his own toshiyori stock. Hence, there were usually more sewanin in Osaka-zumo than there were oyakata. Today, sewanin and wakamono-gashira are no longer eligible to succeed to toshiyori names, even if they were qualified (by having been ranked in Makunouchi for at least one tournament, 20 consecutive tournaments in Juryo or a total of 25 tournaments in Juryo) to become oyakata when they retired from active competition.

Salaries for sewanin and waka-mono-gashira are far from generous. Unlike toshiyori, there are no ranks among sewanin, so salaries increase only when there are general wage increases. All sewanin and waka-mono-gashira retain their *shikona* (fighting name).

Chiho-Sewanin

Chiho-sewanin are not employees of the Sumo Kyokai or of a stable. They are scouts, usually with their own profession, generally located in the countryside. They are affiliated to a given stable and are not necessarily former rikishi.

Managers

Many stablemasters employ a manager to assist with administrative duties in the stable, especially in financial and business matters, while some double as a chauffeur or secretary for the stablemaster. Managers are not employees of the Sumo Kyokai and must be paid from the stablemaster's own funds. Being a stable manager is another possible job for retired wrestlers.

Tokoyama

Tokoyama have a lowly status in the vertical hierarchy of the sumo world but without their presence, sumo would lose much of its appeal. A tokoyama is a sumo hairdresser. This is a year-round profession: all rikishi require their services every day of the year, often more than once a day.

Tokoyama (who must be male) are recruited together with new rikishi and new gyoji, generally at 15 or 16, when they have completed their compulsory education in junior high school. The apprenticeship for a tokoyama is lengthy – the elaborate *oicho-mage* (coiffure) of the sekitori requires about 10 years of training to perfect. A new tokoyama quickly masters the simple *chon-mage*, but he must then make great efforts to learn the skills of fashioning a oicho-mage from his seniors. Each tokoyama has a box of combs, special scented hair grease and unique tools. Senior rikishi often have a favourite tokoyama, who is accustomed to fashioning the rikishi's hair to his specifications. The tokoyama also periodically trims each rikishi's hair to a suitable length.

Tokoyama are not officially employees of the Sumo Kyokai but rather are retained by individual stablemasters. Some stables have more than one tokoyama, others have none and must rely on the goodwill of the hairdresser of a related stable. A few rikishi who have failed to make progress early in their careers but who like the sumo way of life elect to stay with their stable as tokoyama, who retire at the age of 63.

Left Tokoyama (hairdressers) must work when and where they can. During a provincial tour Hoo can be seen having his hair dressed while he reads a book after lunch, before his afternoon nap.

Ozeki Asashio has just had his post-bout bath and is being interviewed while having his hair re-dressed in the normal fashion in the dressing room, prior to getting dressed and going home. During his bout his hair would have been dressed in the shape of a ginko leaf, as is the hair of all rikishi of juryo rank and above.

AWARDS AND PRIZES

The winners of the *sansho*, Mitoizumi and Daijuyama, who were both awarded the Fighting Spirit Award, and (right) Kotogaume, the award for Outstanding Performance. There was no award for Technique at that tournament (May 1988). The winners of the sansho also receive cash prizes of one million yen each.

There are more than 20 different awards and prizes handed out at the end of the tournament to the winner of the top, Makunouchi Division, ranging from the *Tenno Shihai* (Emperor's Cup) to 18 bottles of scotch whisky. Although prizes are given to the winners of all six divisions, winning the Makunouchi Division championship is easily the most prestigious prize in sumo. The winner's name is not only permanently engraved at the bottom of the cup but his larger-than-life-sized portrait is hung inside the Kokugikan and unveiled in a special ceremony. Former grand champion Taiho won

the Emperor's Cup on an all-time record 32 occasions, with the currently active yokozuna Chiyonofuji second with 27. This silver trophy stands 3 feet 2 inches high, has a 12-inch diameter at the base and at 66 pounds it takes a strong man to lift it. A monetary prize of 5 million yen (about $40,000) goes with winning the Emperor's Cup.

Ranking in importance after the Emperor's Cup are the three *Sansho* or Special Prizes, which were instituted in 1947. These are given to top-division wrestlers below the two top ranks of yokozuna and ozeki who have won at least a majority

(eight) of their bouts. The three Sansho are as follows:

Outstanding Performance Award (Shukun-sho) is given to the rikishi who has upset the most yokozuna or combination of yokozuna and ozeki if the latter are title contenders. Former ozeki Asashio holds the all-time record for most Shukun-sho with 10.

Fighting Spirit Prize (Kanto-sho) is given to the rikishi who combines a strong fighting spirit with a good record. This is often a lower-ranked maegashira wrestler who has won more than 10 bouts, but sometimes the Fighting Spirit Prize may be

Above Chiyonofuji accepts the 24th of his 27 Emperor's Cups from Futagoyama Oyakata, the President of the Sumo Association, for winning the Nagoya tournament in July 1988. With it goes a cash prize of five million yen plus innumerable other prizes and honours.

Left After receiving the Cup it is usual for the winner to pose in the dressing room with his supporters, as Chiyonofuji is doing here, and again with them back in heya (see page 60).

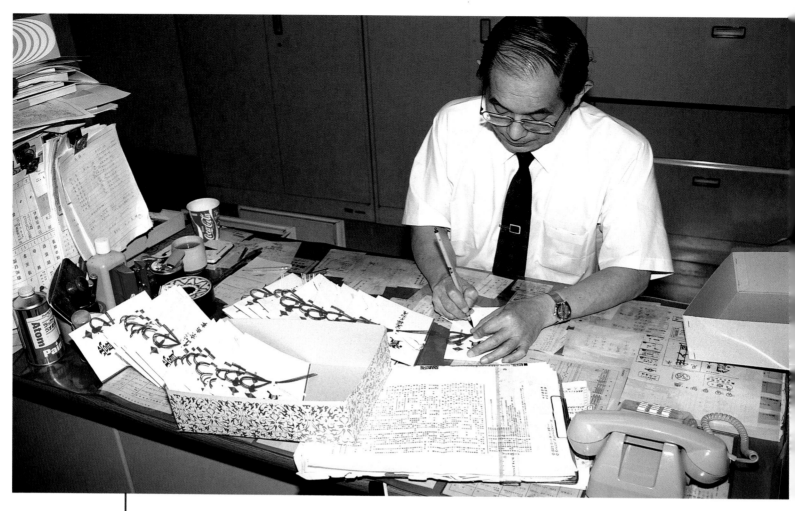

awarded to a high-ranked rikishi below ozeki who has not only demonstrated outstanding fighting spirit but also upset one or two higher-ranked opponents even though he has won only eight or nine bouts during the tournament.

Technique Prize (Gino-sho) is given to the rikishi who has chalked up a reasonably good record, including an upset or two, as a result of either a single finely-honed technique such as pushing, thrusting or throwing or as a result of his technical versatility. Ex-sekiwake Tsurugamine (now Izutsu Oyakata) won the most Gino-sho with 10 and also shares the record for most San-sho of 14 with ex-ozeki Asashio.

Each of these three prizes carries a monetary award of 1 million yen (about $8,000) but sometimes one or more of them may be withheld if there are no worthy candidates. Two rikishi may share the same prize, in which case the prize money is split between them. From 1955 to 1965, one of the Tokyo newspapers sponsored a special prize that was handed out along with the san-sho. It was called the Raiden Prize, based on the prowess of the famous Edo Period ozeki who set the all-time

record for the best winning percentage with .962.

Although it is not symbolically represented in the ring by a trophy, each prestigious *kinboshi* (gold star) earned by a maegashira wrestler for upsetting a grand champion is worth 15,000 yen ($120), which is added to the so-called *kachi-koshi* money that accumulates throughout his career from his debut in the lowest, Jonokuchi Division and which he and all others receive every tournament once they become sekitori (ranked in the two top divisions). For every win over the break-even point, that is, four to seven wins in the four lower divisions and eight to 15 wins in the two top divisions, 500 yen is paid. A veteran wrestler like yokozuna Chiyonofuji receives more than 1 million yen in kachi-koshi money every tournament. As for kinboshi, former Hawaiian sekiwake Takamiyama holds the all-time record with 12, while among currently active rikishi veteran maegashira Ozutsu leads with 10 kinboshi. Some wrestlers, once they hit their stride, come up the ranks so fast that they only have one or two kinboshi: for example, Chiyonofuji has three and fellow-yokozuna Hokutoumi has only one.

Yet lower down in the ranks, Sakahoko has five and Daijuyama seven.

There are also bout prizes called *kensho* put up by sponsors and given to the winners of various individual bouts, even though the advertiser may be sponsoring the bout in which his favourite is defeated. Each advertising sponsor is represented by a banner carried around the ring before the bout by the yobidashi. The origin of kensho can be traced back to the Meiji Period (1867–1912), when they were called *hana*, or flowers. It was then the custom for patrons of the winning rikishi to throw valuables such as clothes and jewellery into the ring at the end of the bout to express their support for him. Some years after this practice was finally stopped in 1909, the awarding of prize-money became formalized as kensho.

Each kensho prize is worth 40,000 yen ($320), although the winner only gets about half of this in an envelope given to him by the referee at the end of the bout. Some of the money is used to pay the tax on the prize, after which time the rikishi receives the rest of it. Former yokozuna Taiho has the record for most kensho in one bout with 26. Because of Emperor Hirohito's death on 7 January 1989, no kensho were presented in the 1989 New Year's Tournament, the first such occurrence since the kensho system was started.

Other awards: The winner of the Makunouchi Division championship not only receives the Emperor's Cup and 5 million yen, but more than 20 other prizes are given to him by a long parade of prize donors. These include the Prime Minister's Cup, Tokyo Governor's Cup (Tokyo basho only) and the Mexico-Japan Friendship Trophy (Tokyo basho only), the Czechoslovakia-Japan Friendship Cup, including a year's supply of beer, the Arab League-Japan Friendship Cup, including a year's supply of gasoline, and the China-Japan Friendship Cup. Two leading Japanese newspapers and the national TV network hand out awards – the *Mainichi Shimbun*, which also throws in a large, framed colour photograph of the winner, the *Tokyo Shimbun* (a plaque) and NHK/ TV, which presents its Gold Cup and 300,000 yen ($2,400).
One of the most popular men at the award ceremonies is American Davey Jones, who has been presenting the Pan American Airways Cup since 1961 and usually elicits several laughs when he attempts to read the citation in the Japanese dialect of the area where the tournament is being held.

Other prizes include a large jar of mushrooms, several thousand pounds of rice, gallons of sake, a year's supply of Coca-Cola, a 2.5-million-yen Baume-Mercier wristwatch and 18 bottles of that ever-popular import in Japan, scotch whisky.

The winners of the Emperor's Cup also have a life-sized portrait presented to them, and this is hung above the balcony seats in the Kokugikan. The presentation of portraits for the previous two tournaments, one in Tokyo and the following provincial tournament, takes place immediately after the dohyo matsuri of each Tokyo tournament. Here are the portraits of Tagaryu, who won in September 1984, and Chiyonfuji, who won in November of the same year.

LIFE AT THE STABLES

ORGANIZATION AND HISTORY

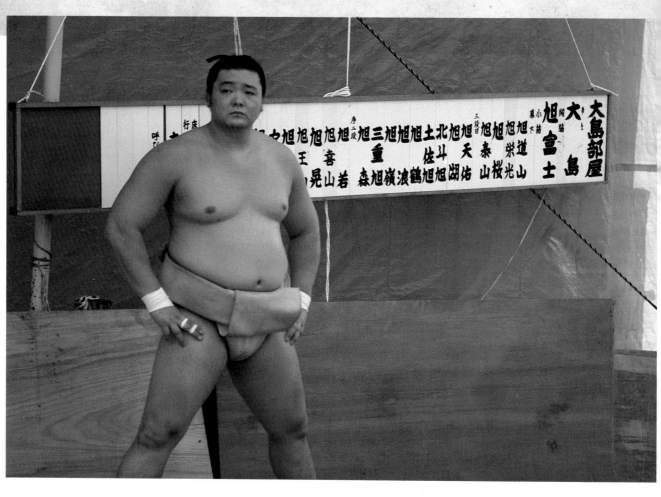

There are 40 *heya*, or sumo stables. The number has been increasing in recent years with more new *oyakata* (elders) reaching affluence at a relatively early age. Establishing a stable is an expensive undertaking; the land and stable building often cost at least 200 million yen ($1.6 million). No rikishi, not even the almost invincible Chiyonofuji, can expect to make the equivalent of a million dollars just from his salary, his ring earnings and retirement allowances. The support of wealthy patrons is essential for the prospective new stablemaster. In theory any oyakata is entitled to establish his own stable, but nearly two-thirds of the elders are coaches in another oyakata's stable. There are two means by which a retired wrestler can become a stablemaster: first, by purchasing his own land and building a stable after receiving permis-

sion from the Japan Sumo Association and from his own stablemaster; or second, through succession when the head of the stable dies, reaches the age of 65 or resigns. An oyakata without adequate funds, however, cannot hope to succeed in becoming a stablemaster.

The origins of sumo stables are obscure. It is safe to say that there have been stables as long as there has been professional sumo. Major stables developed during the latter half of the Edo Period, from the 1750s to the 1860s. Sumo proliferated in the Meiji Period (1867-1912) and by the turn of the 20th century virtually every oyakata was also a stablemaster. The concept of a stable at that time was a far cry from the establishments of today. Every stable now has its own *keiko-ba*, or practice area, while in the Meiji Period only a few of the largest

stables had keikoba, with the average stablemaster having only a few *deshi* (young wrestlers) and merely provided lodging at his own house for his deshi. Rikishi from the small stables had to train at the large stables that had a dohyo, or made do with an improvised dohyo sometimes even in the street.

The number of stables reached an all-time low during the last two years of World War II and the immediate post-war years, during which there was a severe food shortage. Most of the oyakata had almost no money and almost all the stables in the Ryuogoku area had been destroyed in air raids. Numerous small stables were compelled to merge with their large parent heya.

The recovery of the Japanese economy in the 1950s and 1960s increased the number of heya. If the Japanese economy continues to ex-

50

pand at its present rate, with increasing numbers of wealthy businessmen eager to put money forward, there may well be 50 or more stables by the end of this century. Meanwhile, here is a brief rundown on the history of the major stables.

Dewanoumi

Dewanoumi Beya was once the largest stable in sumo with about 150 rikishi. Though much smaller today, it is still prestigious and wealthy. The present Dewanoumi Beya was established by a former maegashira, Hitachiyama Torakichi, in the 1890s. The first Hitachiyama was a heavy drinker and not very ambitious as a stablemaster, but he recruited a nobleman's son who became the second Hitachiyama, an outstanding yokozuna in the early years of this century. Yokozuna Hitachiyama was an exceptional rikishi and one of the greatest stablemasters of his time. He recruited more than 100 rikishi while still an active wrestler himself and made great efforts to lure promising rikishi away from the sumo stables in Osaka and Kyoto. Although Hitachiyama's aggressive expansion of his stable resulted in major disputes with the Osaka sumo world, he became the most powerful figure in Tokyo sumo while still in his 30s. Hitachiyama formally took over as Dewanoumi Oyakata after retiring from active competition in 1914. His operation, backed by some of the extremely wealthy industrial leaders of the time, raised three yokozuna and several ozeki.

Hitachiyama died in 1922 and was succeeded by former komosubi Ryogoku. The stable continued to prosper and had half of the Makunouchi rikishi during the 1920s. However, a strike in 1932 greatly weakened the stable and by the end of the war, it was no longer the

largest in sumo. The present Dewanoumi Oyakata, ex-yokozuna Sadanoyama, is widely viewed as being the strongest candidate to become the next chairman of the Sumo Association, in the footsteps of his two predecessors as Dewanoumi, ex-maegashira Dewanohana and ex-yokozuna Tsunenohana.

Takasago

Takasago Beya was founded in the 1870s by an active rikishi, Takasago Uragoro, who rebelled against the Sumo Association by demanding democratic reforms. The first Takasago returned to the Tokyo Sumo Association's fold after several years of running his own breakaway sumo group and soon became the leading stablemaster. He raised two yokozuna but fell into reactionary ways in his latter years, with his own deshi rebelling against him.

Takasago Beya has been one of the major stables throughout its existence. Maedayama, then a 27-

year-old ozeki who eventually reached yokozuma, took over the heya in 1941. He was an aggressive, often violent man but an outstanding stablemaster after his retirement from active competition. He fought in a powerful thrusting style in his active career, and most Takasago Beya rikishi in the post-war period have been thrusters or pushers. Maedayama died in 1971 and was succeeded by ex-yokozuna Asashio, who was unable to raise a yokozuna of his own and had to be content with developing two ozeki, Asashio and the Samoan-American Konishiki. Ex-yokozuna Asashio died in 1988 and was replaced by the present Takasago, ex-komusubi Fujinishiki.

Futagoyama

Futagoyama Beya, which today leads the Asagaya-area stables, was established by ex-yokozuna Wakanohana I in 1962. Futagoyama's younger brother, ex-ozeki Takanohana, established his own Fujishima Beya

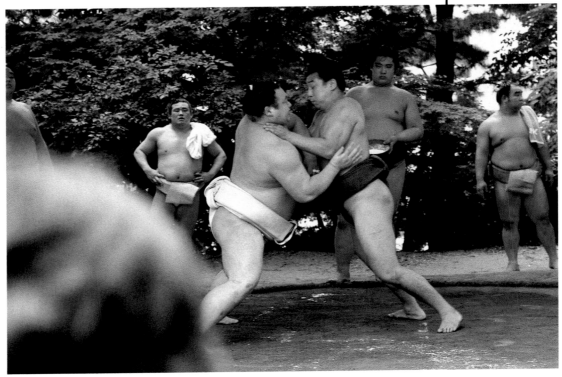

in 1982 in the same area. This now has more rikishi and better prospects in the top-division rikishi Akinoshima and Takanohama than does his elder brother's stable, which includes Daijuyama, Misugisato and Takamisugi in the top division.

Hanaregoma

Hanaregoma Beya, founded by ex-ozeki Kaiketsu, took over all the personnel of Hanakago Beya, from which it and Futagoyama Beya had originated, in December 1985. Hanakago Beya, which had headed the Asagaya stables, was dissolved due to the bankruptcy of its second stablemaster, former yokozuna Wajima. Hanaregoma Beya is now the largest and strongest heya in the Asagaya area with nearly 50 rikishi, including yokozuna Onokuni and two other top-division rikishi Hananoumi and Hananokuni. Futagoyama Oyakata, current chairman of the Sumo Association, is still the leader of the group.

Nishonoseki

Nishonoseki Beya is even older than Dewanoumi Beya and has been one of sumo's leading stables, though it is now declining in importance. The great yokozuna Taiho was a Nishonoseki Beya rikishi and was once expected to take over as stablemaster. A succession dispute took place in 1975, after which sekiwake Kongo took over as stablemaster at the early age of 27. The Futagoyama group of stables in Asagaya still has ties with the Nishonoseki Ichimon, or group of related stables, from which it became independent in the early 1950s. At the beginning of 1989 following the retirement of veteran ex-sekiwake Kiriji, Nishonoseki Beya had not a single rikishi in the top division.

Above Another view of the practice of the rikishi of the Futagoyama-beya.

Right Kasugano Oyakata (at the time President of the Sumo Association) giving advice to some of the makushita and junior rikishi in his heya. During practice sessions many oyakata carry a practice bamboo kendo sword such as Kasugano Oyakata has in his left hand, and use it to chastise and encourage wayward pupils.

STABLE HIERARCHY

Tokitsukaze

The present Tokitsukaze Beya was established by the great pre-war yokozuna Futabayama in 1941. Futabayama developed a very large stable and became the chairman of the Sumo Association and although he developed yokozuna Kagamisato in the 1950s, his stable has been in decline since his death in 1968. The stable once had 15 wrestlers in the top two divisions, but today the ageing Kurama is the only man from the stable with sekitori status. As the wrestlers climb and descend the rankings, so the leading stables flourish and decline over the years.

All sumo stables must have a stable-master. Rikishi must have a stable-master to compete in tournaments; without one the deshi are not recognized as being active wrestlers and therefore cannot compete in a hon-basho. The stablemaster's role is to develop his deshi to their full potential, to instil them with techniques, to monitor their training and provide them with food and lodging. When a stablemaster retires or dies, he must be replaced before the opening of the next tournament at the latest. Some stables consist only of the oyakata (retired wrestlers serving as training coaches) and a few deshi, others have many oyakata,

several referees, ring attendants and other personnel.

There is a strictly maintained order of seniority in every stable. Rikishi have *ani-deshi*, sumo wrestlers who have seniority to them, and *ototo-deshi*, rikishi who are their juniors. The ani-deshi often treat their ototo-deshi roughly, but without this toughening up a sumo wrestler is unlikely to make progress. Though rikishi ranked in the two top divisions have *tsukebito* (attendants) ranked in all the divisions from Makushita and below, ani-deshi ranked in Makushita are often more feared by the youngsters.

Stablemasters who were great yokozuna don't necessarily create the strongest stables. In the past 15 years or so since their formation, Taiho Beya, operated by the grand champion who dominated the 1960s – Taiho – and Kagamiyama Beya, by his chief rival Kashiwado, have been unable to produce any rikishi higher than sekiwake. On the other hand, stables operated by former ozeki in recent years have become extremely strong such as Fujishima Beya run by ex-ozeki Taka-nohana and Oshima Beya by ex-ozeki Asashikuni, both of which have two deshi in the top division. The keys to success are effective leadership, adequate financial backing and a strong scouting organization.

The stablemaster is often greatly assisted by his wife, who is known by the wrestlers in that stable as *okami-san*. She serves as a surrogate mother for the younger rikishi and more often than not helps maintain the stable's finances. The younger oyakata often don their mawashi and train with the active wrestlers in their stable, while older oyakata may concentrate on administrative duties within the Sumo Association. Referees and ring attendants also provide support in handling the administration of a stable.

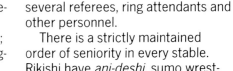

TRAINING

Although sumo training consists almost entirely of traditional training methods handed down over the centuries, a gradually increasing number of sumo wrestlers are starting to incorporate such modern methods as weight training, jogging or fast-paced long-distance walking.

Yokozuna Chiyonofuji took up weight training because of the numerous shoulder dislocations that he suffered in the lower ranks. Although at 270 pounds he is one of the lightest rikishi in the top division, he has been the strongest man in sumo for several years. He is also one of the fastest and most agile wrestlers, having refused to accept the traditional dictum that to become strong, you have to keep adding more and more weight. As a new type of role model, Chiyonofuji may have shown today's youth in Japan that they can become successful by following in his footsteps

rather than those of 448-pound yokozuna Onokuni. Former grand champion Wajima, who retired at the beginning of the 1980s and was the first former collegiate sumotori to reach the highest rank, used to do a lot of jogging to stay in shape, while yokozuna Takanosato, one of Chiyonofuji's strongest rivals in the early 1980s, lifted weights so much he eventually became muscle-bound, leaving him with a very strong but inflexible body.

The rikishi from Hawaii in Azumazeki Beya (run by ex-sekiwake Takamiyama from Maui Island) – Takamikuni, Takamio and Akebono – go to the weight training gym of Dr Bob Beveredge in Ebisu, Tokyo, where they work out on weekends when they are in Tokyo. Azumazeki Oyakata, familiarly known as Jesse, has instituted a fast-walking programme for his deshi, requiring them to cover a certain distance

within a certain time. Sometimes they may join ozeki Konishiki for power-lifting practice at a nearby gym in Okachi-machi, Tokyo. Konishiki is also a keen swimmer and even dancer despite his huge bulk, often gracing the floor of Tokyo discos.

Stable training begins as early as 4.30 or 5.00 am for the newest members of the stable, with others rising later in accordance with their increase in rank until the stable's yokozuna, ozeki or highest-ranked sekitori is reached. The senior wrestler generally lies undisturbed until about 7 am. The most common type of training is a sort of king of the mountain competition referred to as *moshi-ai*. The winner takes on all comers in the stable ring. As soon as the bout is over, the other deshi waiting around the outside edge of the ring rush up to the winner, each appealing to him for the right to be

At Kasugano-beya a new boy gets help with *matawari* from an oyakata coach in mufti on the left, Tochitsukasa on the right, and another junior riskishi behind him.

Yokozuna Onokuni
squats outside during
practice, which last
from five or six o'clock
until about ten or
eleven.

Two junior rikishi prac-
tise at the Takasago-
beya in Tokyo. This is
typical of the Tokyo
headquarters of all the
heya. On the wall on
the left are the names
of all the members of
the heya written on
tablets that can be
moved from right to
left as the rikishi move
up and down the ban-
zuke. High up on the
wall facing is a small
Shinto altar, to which
rikishi bow when they
first enter and finally
leave the practice area.

his next opponent. The other type of practice bout is known as *sanban-geiko*, which is usually restricted to sekitori or the top two or four deshi in the stable and involves 12 to 15 bouts between two wrestlers.

Training usually tapers off two or three days before the start of a tournament, so that many top-rankers only do light practice on the Friday and Saturday leading up to the opening of the basho or when recovering from an injury. When they practise with some of the lower-ranked deshi in their stable, this is called *anma*, or getting a massage. Other types of training include *tsuriashi* which involves charging across the ring to the edge from a crouching position and pushing an imaginary opponent across the ring, stopping short at the edge. There's also *matawari* – doing the sumo splits. This entails sitting and stretching your legs outward as far apart as possible and then bending forward until you touch your forehead and even your chest on the dirt floor. If the young sumotori can't make it all the way down, one of the oyakata or a senior rikishi climbs on his back and forces him down. This often brings tears of pain to the youth's eyes.

Then there are the traditional shiko and teppo training. *Shiko* is alternately stamping your foot into the clay for a hundred times or more. Several stables arrange their young deshi in rows at the end of the day's training and require them to do shiko, with the sumotori taking turns in calling out the stamping by number – *ichi, ni, san, shi, go* and so on up to 10. Shiko is done to strengthen the hips and legs. The former Hawaiian wrestler Takamiyama recalls that it sometimes became so painful in his first couple of years of sumo that he could hardly drag himself up the stairs to his bed at night.

Every stable has a big wooden pole in one corner, and slapping this pole is called *teppo*. This is done rhythmically, alternately slapping the pole with each hand and stepping forward with each foot on the same side that you slap the pole, thus allowing you to put your body into each blow. Though this exercise is a must for thrusters and pushers to toughen and enlarge their hands and to develop the rhythm essential to that kind of attack, it often leaves their hands bruised and numb.

A leg-stretching exercise termed *shinkyaku* is also important to limber up before a bout. This involves squatting and fully extending one leg and then the other from side to side, alternately back and forth. The sumotori usually presses down on his leg as he extends it outward. A similar exercise is done from a squatting position, with the legs stretched outward as in matawari. The sumotori then bends his torso forward along the line of each leg in turn, extending his arms outward to touch his toes.

Daily practice sessions usually end up with a rugged type of training called *butsukari-geiko*, although some stables follow this up with group foot stamping exercises. A rikishi pushes his partner back and forth across the ring to strengthen his pushing power and sometimes rolls him into the dirt to improve his ability to take a fall without injury. Charging forward, colliding with an opponent and pushing him out of the ring – this is sumo's most fundamental technique. Through constant repetition of this severe training, a rikishi gradually increases his power.

Butsukari-geiko, usually the final exercise after sanban-geiko, and the most gruelling. Onishiki (right, now Yamashina Oyakata and a coach at Dewanoumi-beya) is 'lending his chest' to a junior rikishi who is trying to push him back across the dohyo. It is an exercise guaranteed to extend the fittest, but also helps the rikishi being pushed.

EATING AND DRINKING

Sumo wrestlers eat the same traditional mid-day boiled stew, *chanko-nabe*, day in and day out almost without change throughout their entire careers. (Confusingly, the word *chanko* is also the term that rikishi use to refer to food in general.) There is no such thing as breakfast in a sumo stable. The day's first meal comes around 11.30 am after training is over and the rikishi have taken a bath. There aren't enough tables to accommodate everyone in the stable at once, except in the very small ones, therefore the rikishi and the others living in the stable such as the stablemaster, training coaches, stable manager and assistants, referees, ring attendants and hair dressers must eat in shifts in accordance with their rank. Hence the stablemaster and training coaches as well as the senior rikishi eat first, followed by those of lower and lower rank until at last the *shin-deshi* (new stable wrestlers) are reached. By this time, most of the meat or fish is gone and only the bones and a few scraps of vegetables remain along with the broth and, of course, rice. If a wrestler is disgruntled with his skimpy portion, he can remedy the situation by continuing to rise up the ranking ladder because the higher he is ranked, the sooner he eats.

Chanko-nabe consists of a variety of vegetables — cabbage, carrots, potatoes, radishes and spinach as well as tofu (soybean curd) and either fish or some kind of meat, usually chicken or pork. Most of the foreign sumo wrestlers, even the Hawaiians and Samoans, have great difficulty learning to eat fish chanko several times a week. It took Takamiyama of Hawaii two or three years before he could stomach such an unremitting diet of fish. The young wrestlers in the stable are assigned to help the chief cook prepare the stew. They even have to go out shopping for the ingredients and then come back, wash the food, chop it up into the proper size for eating and make the broth from bonito flakes, chicken bones and various types of seasoning.

Some stables try to force-feed their most promising deshi, interrupting their morning training from time to time and making them eat a big bowl of rice. Top-division veteran Ozutsu of Taiho Beya recalls that for a time during his early years in sumo he was downing a staggering 20 bowls of rice a day, including the rice he had with his chanko-nabe.

The evening meal consists of ordinary fare, either Japanese or western style. Most of the sekitori will be gone by this time, either invited out by some patron or relaxing at home if he is married. The lower-ranked deshi may even have some more chanko-nabe if there's any left over from the noon meal but more likely they will eat something like instant noodles, Japanese-style curry rice or some other inexpensive, easily-prepared food. When it comes to eating and drinking, many sumo wrestlers could easily put to shame such famous gluttons as Diamond Jim Brady. In fact, their gargantuan size can be traced directly to their extraordinary eating habits. Former grand champion Yoshibayama once polished off six dozen bowls of noodles at one sitting and another wolfed down 36 box lunches.

Sumo wrestlers are noted for phenomenal feats of drinking, as well. On a tour of Australia presented as a prize to the winner of the New Year's Tournament in the mid-1960s, former grand champion Taiho, a giant of over six feet and 330 pounds, quaffed a prodigious quantity of beer, easily outdrinking an Australian rugby player, who was the team's drinking champ. Ex-yokozuna Kitanoumi (5 feet 11 inches, 375 pounds) who flourished in the late 1970s and early 1980s,

was also famous for his stupendous eating and drinking habits. It was not unusual for him to empty three bottles of whisky during a night of drinking. Former Hawaiian sumo wrestler Takamiyama, a 440-pound colossus, once admitted that he drank 38 quart bottles of beer in an all-night drinking session with his stablemates.

Mitoizumi (left) and Ozeki Asashio have just finished practice, had their daily bath, and are now, at about eleven o'clock, having their first meal of the day with some of their friends or supporters, waited upon by the young rikishi who stand behind them. Usually only the Oyakata and sekitori or maybe an important member of a support group (koenkai) can or will invite people to eat with them, and to be invited to eat is a great honour.

FINANCING A STABLE

All 40 sumo stables receive allowances from the Sumo Association to help defray expenses for food, maintenance and clothing. The stablemaster is given a monthly allowance for each rikishi, based on his rank and a lesser amount for other personnel in the stable. However, these subsidies from the Sumo Association are not adequate to operate a stable. Most stablemasters own their stable building and its land, and thus rent, which is exorbitant in the Tokyo area, is almost never a problem.

Rikishi plough their way through at least twice the average Japanese food intake, so feeding the wrestlers is the greatest daily expense a stablemaster faces. Food and beverage costs are kept in check by purchasing wholesale. Although almost all of the lower-ranked wrestlers participate in preparing the sumo stew on a rota basis, most stables designate one or two rikishi to buy the essential ingredients. This may entail visits to the Tsukiji Fish Market every morning.

The promotion of a wrestler to Juryo for the first time is an event for celebration but it also entails considerable expense. A new *kesho-mawashi*, or embroidered silk apron, costs at least 1 million yen ($8,000), as does the *shimekomi* or silk belt used by sekitori. Another 500,000 yen ($4,000) or so is needed to

Left On the last night of a tournament a party is held. Kokonoe Oyakata (former yokozuna Kitanofuji, left of Chiyohofuji) and some prominent supporters are filling a large sake bowl so as to toast Chiyohofuji after his 21st championship win in July 1987.

Above Hanaregoma Oyakata (left) and his supporters are toasting Onokuni on his promotion to ozeki in July 1985. On the table is a carp, a fish always eaten on auspicious occasions in Japan and China; in front of the table are the microphones used for the interview which always accompanies any event of importance in the sporting world. The *tsuna* (ceremonial rope) that encircles the yokozuna's girth when he performs his dohyo-iri is what distinguishes him on the surface from the ozeki. The tsuna is made anew just before each Tokyo tournament by the combined efforts of the whole ichimon or group of related heya.

purchase a new *montsuki* (crested formal kimono used by sekitori on formal occasions). All told, a minimum of 3-4 million yen ($24,000-32,000) is spent for each new sekitori when he is promoted to Juryo.

A still greater sum of money is required when a wrestler is promoted to yokozuna. The *tsuna* or great white hawser worn by the yokozuna during his entrance to the ring is made at the stable in a combined effort of all its rikishi. The hemp and steel wire used to construct the tsuna may cost a couple of hundred thousand yen but much of that sum is provided by the Sumo Association. The average new yokozuna is presented with at least six new sets of kesho-mawashi for his dohyo-iri, with each set consisting of three ceremonial aprons, one for the yokozuna himself and one each for his *tachimochi* (swordbearer) and *tsuyuharai* (herald). A minimum of 18 or so new kesho-mawashi must be ordered; as the yokozuna's kesho-mawashi are of the highest quality, the total expenditure on the aprons is at least 50 million yen ($400,000). Furthermore, a party to commemorate the promotion is held at a first-class hotel in Tokyo, attended by at least 1,000 guests. The minimum cost of the party is

Asashio making *tegata* (hand prints), which are given out to supporters at parties, with the rikishi's signature written in Chinese characters with a brush. Although retired rikishi will still sign autographs, tegata are generally made only while a rikishi is actively wrestling.

usually a staggering 70-80 million yen ($560,000–640,000).

Where does all this money come from? The Sumo Association's subsidies are modest; the stablemasters may be wealthy but not to the extent of buying kesho-mawashi and funding extraordinarily expensive parties. It is the *koenkai*, or supporting associations, that provide all the money for these expenses. All stables must have a koenkai in order to survive. The koenkai are generally headed by wealthy businessmen and politicians. The membership is also open to the general public – at a price. The koenkai of the larger stables or of stables housing yoko-zuna or ozeki are the most wealthy and the most expensive to join. Most wrestlers in the two top divisions also have their own personal koenkai. Many stables and some individual wrestlers have koenkai in Tokyo as well as in Osaka, Nagoya and Fukuoka, where tournaments are held in March, July and November, respectively.

The monetary support of koenkai is not limited just to buying new aprons. The most affluent koenkai also present rikishi with large sums of money when they win championships or merely for achieving *kachi-koshi*, a winning record at a tournament. The average fighter in the two top divisions receives far more from his own koenkai or from his stable's koenkai than he does from the Sumo Association. A wealthy koenkai also helps retiring rikishi to buy their *toshiyori kabu*

(retired, elder name). This may cost up to 100 million yen ($800,000), so rikishi from a stable with a large, generous koenkai have a decided advantage in remaining in the sumo world after their retirement from active competition.

Rikishi must, of course, reciprocate the generosity of their koenkai. The simplest favour granted to koenkai members is producing *tegata* (signed handprints). Tegata of the leading rikishi are much coveted. Yokozuna Chiyonofuji, the most

popular rikishi for almost a decade, is said to have produced several hundred thousand of his tegata. Although his prints are the most common, they are also the most sought after. When a senior rikishi retires, he personally visits all his major koenkai members to thank them for their generosity and perhaps tacitly to ask for their support in building his own stable. A few of the most generous supporters may be given some of his kesho-mawashi as mementoes.

LEISURE AND LOVE

Once training is over and they have bathed and eaten chanko-nabe, nearly all sumo wrestlers customarily take a long afternoon nap to give the food time to digest and convert itself into extra poundage. Married wrestlers live outside the stable in their own apartment, although most of them eat the mid-day meal of stew before going home. Some of the more popular rikishi may have such a busy schedule, except during tournaments, that they go out for both lunch and dinner with members of their koenkai and other wealthy patrons.

Once they eat and take their afternoon nap, the sekitori (wrestlers in the two top divisions) can do pretty much as they choose,

although they are obliged to spend time with the stable's patrons when requested to do so. The lower-ranked rikishi have so many chores and other duties to take care of that they have very little time of their own. They must obtain permission from the stablemaster to go out, especially at night. Moreover, most of them have only the pocket money the oyakata gives them and could not afford to go out drinking even if allowed to.

The usual practice for those inviting yokozuna and other top-ranked wrestlers out for dinner and an evening of drinking is to pay them for the privilege of their company. The money is wrapped in a special kind of paper and the amount

depends on the rank of the wrestler. An invitation to a star like Chiyonofuji may cost at least $2,000.

Almost half of the wrestlers in the top division are married. Sumo wrestlers, kabuki actors and geisha were regarded as the three flowers of the Edo Period (1603–1867). Indeed, some sumo romances still evoke as much curiosity and excitement today as the amorous adventures of movie stars and pop singers. But sumo and sex is a magic combination that sets it apart from the passionate entanglements of other celebrities, perhaps because of the sharp contrast between the burly, top-knotted rikishi and their petite, modern-minded brides. Three small examples of romantic

Marriage is impossible until a rikishi has become a sekitori, since before that he has no regular salary. The higher in rank the sekitori, the more elaborate will be the wedding ceremony. Here Ozeki Asahifuji and his bride, flanked by the go-between, their parents and Asahifuji's boss, Ushima Oyakata and his wife, welcome guests at their wedding reception at the Hotel New Otani in Tokyo in January 1989.

rikishi will suffice.

In 1963, a promising, 21-year-old wrestler in the top division named Sakahoko ran off with a 44-year-old bar hostess from Kyoto who had been following him from tournament to tournament. Former ozeki Taka-nohana, one of the most popular rikishi of the 1960s, took the plunge at the tender age of 19 after carrying on a torrid love affair with actress Noriko Fujita. When former yokozuna Taiho was single, he was inundated by hundreds of letters every week from female fans. And when he married an innkeeper's daughter in 1967, their nuptuals were accompanied by the plushest, most expensive wedding reception in Japanese history.

THE KOKUGIKAN

On the other side of the Sumida River from downtown Tokyo next to Ryogoku Station stands an imposing, green-roofed structure crowned by a golden crest. In front of it is erected during the three Tokyo tournaments a tall, wooden framework called a *yagura* with colourful banners fluttering on all sides like some ancient watchtower on a battlefield of opposing Japanese armies. This is Japan's National Sumo Arena, known to most sumo fans simply as the Kokugikan. Opened in January 1985 for the New Year's Tournament, the $40 million Kokugikan seats 11,000 spectators and is equipped with machinery for raising and lowering the dohyo as well as the *yakata*, the two-ton, Shinto-style roof that hangs over the ring.

Several special rooms are located in the first basement, including two dressing rooms for the rikishi, the judges' room, press room, the sumo clinic together with the Sports Medicine Research Centre, the Grand Hall and facilities for the Sumo Service Company. On the main floor are the entrances to the arena with the dohyo at the apex of the raked seating area with its *masu-seki* (traditional four-seat boxes) and western-style boxes circling the first-floor seats. The Sumo Association's offices are also on the first floor along with the sumo museum and other facilities. The Emperor's

spacious royal box (used not only by the imperial family but also by foreign dignitaries) is located on the second floor along with the *isu-seki*, or single seats, space for the wheel-chairs of the handicapped and a restaurant specializing in traditional Japanese food. Just off the corridor running around the arena area are the *chaya* – 20 tea-house stalls that handle the tickets for the four-seat boxes and provide souvenirs as well as food and drink catering facilities for customers in the sumo boxes. There are also various shops along the corridor selling snacks, soft drinks and beer, souvenirs, sumo video tapes, modern sumo wood-block prints and such like. Public telephones and rest-rooms are also

located in this part of the building.

The first permanent Kokugikan opened in 1909 next to the Ekoin Buddhist Temple in Tokyo's Ryogoku section; at that time sumo underwent a major reorganization, including the institution of several new rules and the official recognition of

street the old pre-war Kokugikan was in the last stages of demolition. And meanwhile at the arena at Kuramae preparations were being made for the Summer Tournament, held in May.

Today only one Kokugikan remains. Its predecessor at Kuramae was torn down to make way for a modern sewage-treatment plant, while the site of the old Ryogoku Kokugikan next to the Ekoin Temple is now serving as a temporary parking lot pending construction of a new building there. The allied powers repaired the old, war-ravaged Ryogoku Kokugikan during the Occupation of Japan and two Aki Basho were held there in November 1945 and 1946. In the latter tournament, the allies had the diameter of the dohyo temporarily widened to about 16 feet to make the bouts last longer but this change was quickly dropped. In December 1945 the allies expropriated the Kokugikan, forcing the Sumo Kyokai to hold the tournaments elsewhere until the new Kuramae Kokugikan was opened as a temporary structure in 1950 and completed in 1954. The old Ryogoku Kokugikan eventually became the Nihon University Auditorium.

the title of yokozuna for the first time. But eight years later it burned down.

The second Kokugikan opened in 1920 on the site of the first and, despite the Great Tokyo Earthquake of 1923 and World War II bombing, it survived (though unused for basho

after 1946) until the third Kokugikan was built across the Sumida River in the Kuramae district in 1954. For a few weeks in April 1983, there were three kokugikan, all within a mile of each other. While the foundations of the Ryogoku Kokugikan were being laid, just five minutes' walk down the

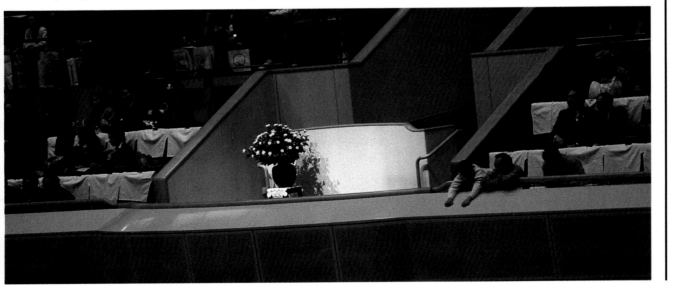

THE JAPAN SUMO ASSOCIATION

The Nihon Sumo Kyokai, or the Japan Sumo Association, is the sole governing body of professional sumo. Though many of its operations resemble those of a business corporation, the association is actually registered with the Japanese government's Ministry of Education as a non-profit entity. The Japan Sumo Association came into being in its present form in December 1925, when the Ministry of Education accepted the organization's articles of incorporation. Though the association has existed for only 64 years in its present form, its origins lie in the professional sumo organization that developed in Edo (now Tokyo) in the middle of the 18th century. In 1925 there was still a separate professional sumo world with its own governing body in Osaka. The Osaka wrestlers were generally inferior to those in the capital and by 1925 the Osaka Sumo Association was nearly bankrupt, with dwindling attendances at tournaments. In 1926, the Osaka Sumo Association had little alternative but to merge with the Tokyo body; sealing this new unity, 17 Osaka oyakata joined the 88 oyakata in Tokyo.

The Sumo Association is comprised of and operated by former senior rikishi who hold *toshiyori* (elder names). There is a total of 105 toshiyori names, while two great yokozuna – Taiho and Kitanoumi – retain their fighting names as elders in the association. The Sumo Kyokai is an all-powerful body; it has total control of all tournaments, it promulgates and enforces rules pertaining to sumo bouts, attire and the conduct of rikishi. The popularization of the sport is a further responsibility.

The management strategy of the Sumo Association is something of a paradox. Its financial planning is very shrewd, with a high profit level consistently maintained. When the

new Kokugikan was built in the early 1980s, it is said that the association was able to pay the 15 billion yen ($120 million) construction cost in cash. On the other hand, sumo's governing body is extremely conservative, some would even say feudalistic. Although elections for all posts are theoretically mandated once every two years, actually everything is decided in advance when the most senior elders reach tacit agreement on new appointments. A balance of power between the *ichimon* (groups of related stables) is maintained, with at least one senior representative from each ichimon sitting on the board of directors.

The present chairman of the

Sumo Kyokai is 60-year-old Futagoyama, the former yokazuna Wakanohana I who won 10 championships during his heyday in the 1950s. He succeeded his old ring rival Tochinishiki (Kasugano Oyakata) as chairman in 1988 and is expected to head the sumo world for two two-year terms until 1992. Unlike most former yokozuna of his age, Futagoyama is relatively small and is in robust health. He is the first oyakata from his ichimon – centred in the Asagaya area on the opposite side of Tokyo from the Ryogoku sumo heartland – to assume the top post in the Sumo Association. He has been an extraordinarily successful stablemaster, having raised two

Every year the leading officials of the Sumo Association and the sanyaku make a pilgrimage to the Grand Shrine at Ise, where the dohyo-iri are performed. Here they pose for a photo.

yokozuna and two ozeki to date. A conservative much in the mould of his predecessor, Kasugano, Futagoyama has placed stress on more rigorous training.

The Sumo Association has a rigidly structured hierarchy. The oyakata most recently retired from active competition perform such humble functions as manning the ticket gate during tournaments and providing security. More senior oyakata serve as managers of small subsections, from which they may advance to the prestigious post of *shimpan*, or judge. Oyakata generally withdraw from the Judging Division when they reach their late 50s and take less demanding posts. Position in the Sumo Kyokai is not determined solely by age or the number of years as an oyakata. Prowess in the ring counts for a good deal once the wrestler's career is over. Former rikishi taking over a major stable as (well as) former yokozuna and ozeki tend to advance much faster up the ladder of elders than the average wrestler in the top division.

The Sumo Museum

The Sumo Museum is just off the entrance hall to the Kokugikan. The museum is headed on an acting basis by Kasugano Oyakata, the former yokozuna Tochinishiki who headed the Sumo Association as chairman from 1974 to 1988. Kasugano will become the director of the museum in 1990, when he reaches

Futagoyama Oyakata, President of the Sumo Association, presents the top rikishi to the spectators on the opening day of a tournament. He is flanked on his right by yokozuna Hokutoumi and Chyonofuji and on his left by yokozuna Onokuni and ozeki Hokutenyu; behind are ozeki Konishiki, Asahifuji and Asashio.

65 and retires from being a stablemaster.

Until 1954, there was no sumo museum. During the construction of the old Kokugikan at Kuramae in the early 1950s, the Sumo Association made great efforts to acquire relics of the early yokozuna to supplement its own archives, most of which had been lost or damaged in the Great Tokyo Earthquake of 1923 and the air raids near the end of World War II. The Sumo Museum's collection of memorabilia is impressive but space limitations dictate that only a very small selection of the total collection can be displayed at any one time. Nevertheless, one can gain an insight into the sport's long history.

The Origins of Sumo

The earliest origins of sumo are obscure. Forms of wrestling that resemble sumo existed in ancient Egypt, Babylon, India, China, Mongolia and Korea. There is evidence that a primitive form of sumo was present in Japan more than 2,000 years ago. Although there are tales about sumo in Japan's ancient mythology, it wasn't until the Nara Period in 734 that the sport was exhibited before the imperial court. Sumo exhibitions were performed for the emperors and later for the *shogunate* long before the sport became professional. Indeed, professional sumo dates back only to the 17th century.

Initially, professional sumo tournaments were organized in Osaka and Kyoto, while in Edo (now Tokyo) – the seat of the shogunate – the authorities often suppressed sumo tournaments on grounds that they were an unfavourable influence on public order. Finally, at the end of the 17th century, the shogunate began to permit regular sumo tournaments in Edo under strict rules on techniques and the organization of the rikishi.

Banzuke, or ranking lists, began to appear regularly in Kyoto at the end of the 1600s, and in Edo around 1720. At first, only one banzuke was made, on a wooden placard, but the increasing popularity of professional sumo tournaments soon brought the need for printed banzuke. Professional sumo centred on Kyoto and Osaka until the 1760s. In 1769, a powerful 19-year-old called Tanikaze Kajinosuke – known at that time as Dategaseki – was given an honorary ozeki rank at Edo. The youth was not highly regarded when he made his debut, but he soon attained near-invincibility and went on to dominate the sumo world for more than a quarter of a century. As his base was in Edo, the shogunate capital became sumo's mecca. In 1789, Tanikaze and his rival, Onogawa Kisaburo, were jointly honoured with the rank of yokozuna.

Tanikaze died in 1795, while his ageing rival Onogawa continued to compete into the early years of the 19th century. In the meantime, another extremely powerful rikishi, Raiden Tamaemon, appeared at Edo. He lost only 10 bouts in more than 25 years in the Makunouchi division and is still regarded by some as the strongest rikishi of all time. Despite his phenomenal record he was never promoted to yokozuna – some say he was regarded as being *too* strong, but more likely he lacked the influence or the right connections to gain the honorary elite status.

Two tournaments were held at Edo each year. Generally in January and May, these were almost always at the Ekoin, a Buddhist temple in Ryogoku. The Osaka and Kyoto sumo authorities, who were independent of the Edo sumo organizers, both staged one annual tournament, managing to attract most of the rikishi who appeared in Edo.

The Decline of Feudal Japan

The collapse of the shogunate at Edo in 1867 brought a period of great turmoil to the nation and sumo was not exempt from this. The Meiji Emperor moved from Kyoto to Edo, which was renamed Tokyo. Eager to westernize in a hurry, the new government decreed that the traditional top-knots worn by men would have to go. Though sumo wrestlers were granted immunity from the hair-cutting order, the warning signs were out and, for a time, there were fears that sumo would disappear with the westernization of Japan.

In the 1870s the popularity of the sport was at its nadir. The Osaka and Kyoto sumo associations staged tournaments with rikishi who no longer participated in Tokyo events. In 1873, a group of Tokyo rikishi seceded from the Sumo Association after being rebuffed in an attempt to introduce at least some degree of democratic reform to the sumo world.

Sumo did not fully recover from the confusion attendant on the collapse of the feudalistic regime until the turn of the 20th century. This revival was assisted by the tremendous interest generated by two great yokozuna, Hitachiyama and Umegatani II, who drew capacity crowds to the Tokyo tournaments. With this boost to their revenues the Tokyo sumo authorities gradually began to recover financially and in 1909 the first permanent Kokugikan, or indoor sumo arena, was completed near the old Ekoin Temple. Destroyed by fire in 1917, this arena was rebuilt two years later. Hitachiyama and Umegatani II retired in 1914 and 1915, respectively, with the prodigiously strong but uncharismatic Tachiyama taking their places as the strongest rikishi.

Progress Towards Unity

The independent sumo worlds in Kyoto and Osaka faded after the turn of the 20th century. The sport in Kyoto fell apart after its leading rikishi were lured by a British promoter to stage an exhibition in 1910. The Kyoto contingent was stranded in Europe after it exhausted its funds. Many of the leading Kyoto rikishi were never to return to Japan. In Osaka, sumo struggled on the verge of bankruptcy for two decades, at times finding itself in hock to *yakuza* (gangsters). In 1926, the Tokyo and Osaka associations merged into the present Japan Sumo Association based in Tokyo.

The Sumo Association nearly fell apart when more than half of the Makunouchi and Juryo rikishi formed their own group in the Tenryu Strike of 1932. The vacuum caused by the strike brought many junior wrestlers to the top division and one, Futabayama Sadaji, became a living legend. Futabayama

leapt to prominence in 1936 as a maegashira. He was unbeaten for three years and during that time rose from third-ranked maegashira to yokozuna. Futabayama's 69-bout winning streak came to an end in January 1939. This record has never been surpassed and may indeed stand for all time. Futabayama's loss to little-regarded maegashira Akinoumi was arguably the greatest upset in the history of the sport. Futabayama's career paralleled Japan's rise and fall as a military power. He had his last good year in 1943, faded in 1944, and retired in the first post-war tournament in November 1945. The great Tokyo air raids of March 1945 burned almost all of the sumo stables to the ground but, though severely damaged, the sturdy Kokugikan survived.

The Post-War Period

Two skilful technicians, Tochinishiki and Wakanohana I, did much to revive the popularity of sumo during the 1950s. Both men were to become chairman of the Sumo Association. Soon, more personalities began to emerge. In 1960, a lanky teenager named Taiho made a sensationally impressive debut in Makunouchi and by the end of the following year he had risen to yokozuna. Another young rikishi, Kashiwado, was promoted to sumo's highest rank at the same time. The era of Taiho and Kashiwado extended throughout the 1960s, with Kashiwado retiring in 1969 and his rival in 1971. Taiho won a total of 32 championships, an all-time record that current yokozuna Chiyonofuji seems to be gunning for.

In July 1972, Takamiyama, an American from the Hawaiian island of Maui, became the first foreign rikishi to win the Emperor's Cup, symbol of a tournament championship. The rise of Takamiyama in addition to overseas tours during

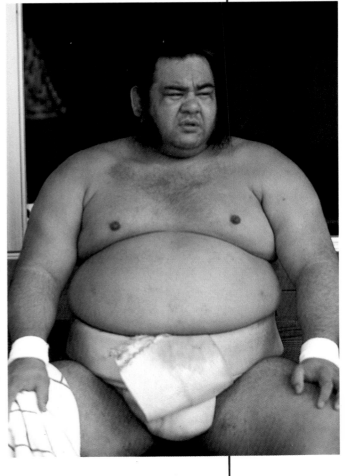

the 1960s and 1970s to California, Hawaii, Russia and China did much to spread the popularity of sumo internationally. Kitanoumi and former college champion Wajima were the outstanding yokozuna of the 1970s, with the former winning 24 championships – the third best record after Taiho and Chiyonofuji. The decline of Kitanoumi in the early 1980s corresponded with the rise of Chiyonofuji, the muscular lightweight superstar who continues to dominate sumo today. Sumo, with its lavish new Kokugikan opened in January 1985, continues to be popular in Japan even though baseball draws larger crowds. Having survived for more than 2,000 years, there is every reason to believe that sumo will flourish for many more centuries.

Takamiyama (now Azumazeki Oyakata), sitting on the verandah of the temple in the outskirts of Nagoya at which Takasago-beya stay for the Nagoya tournament in July, a year or so before he retired in the autumn of 1984. He now has his own heya and some promising rikishi.

THE SUMO CLINIC

Because of their diet and strenuous training many rikishi suffer from internal ailments. Former Yokozuna Takanosato (now Naruto Oyakata) fought diabetes to reach the top rank in sumo, and wrote a book telling how he did it. Here he talks to a fan at the party given by his heya after he won the championship in July 1983.

The Sumo Association has maintained a clinic for conducting regular physical examinations of the wrestlers since 1957. New sumo recruits are also checked here to ensure that they meet the minimum qualifications to enter the professional ranks. Before a new sumo recruit can enter a stable, he must meet the minimum qualifications set for new entrants: 171 cm (5 ft 7 in) and 70 kg (155 lb) for those under 18 years of age, 174 cm (5 ft 8 in) and 75 kg (165 lb) for those 18 and over. The clinic's head, Dr Yamada, stresses the importance of physical examinations since the rigorous daily training often results in high blood pressure, inflammation of the joints and strained muscles. The massive intake of food also produces a variety of ailments.

Tamanoumi, a 27-year-old grand champion and seemingly in good health, died suddenly in October 1971 of a heart attack a few days after a routine appendectomy. He was at least 100 pounds overweight at the time. Many of these ailments are chronic and when added to retirement at an early age, inevitably leading to a drastic curtailment of the vigorous lifestyle, they combine to send sumo wrestlers to an early grave.

Every rikishi undergoes a physical check-up at the clinic once a year. Dr Yamada indicates that the most common ailments are diabetes, gout, high blood pressure and liver trouble. Common injuries include sprains, dislocations, joint separations, bruises, contusions and an occasional fracture. Yokozuna Chiyonofuji has suffered several shoulder dislocations, injuries that have sidelined him in three tournaments over the past six years. The last such withdrawal was in the 1989 May Tournament. In fact, Chiyo took up weight training for just that reason – to strengthen his shoulders against dislocations.

Chiyo's stablemate and fellow-yokozuna, Hokutoumi, injured his lower back and waist so severely while limbering up for a bout on the 14th day of the 1988 Summer Tournament that he was forced to sit out the next three tournaments. One-time sekiwake Mitoizumi suffered such a bad sprain in his opening-day bout in November 1988 with yokozuna Onokuni that he had to pull out of the tournament the next day and even missed the following January Tournament. Maegashira Kirinishiki fractured the back of his right hand in the 1988 May Tournament and then aggravated the injury so that he too was unable to compete in the 1989 New Year's Tournament.

There is only one recorded case of a sumo injury resulting in death and that was back in the Edo Period some 150 to 200 years ago. In fact, one could probably count on the fingers of one hand the total number of permanently crippling injuries that have occurred in sumo – a surprising fact, considering the spectacle of mountainous men hurling themselves against each other.

Most of the more serious problems arise after the rikishi retire. Only about six years after he retired at 31, the great former yokozuna Taiho (now Taiho Oyakata and master of Taiho Stable) collapsed from a high-blood-pressure stroke that paralysed his left side. But with physiotherapy treatment, he was able completely to regain the use of every part of his body except his left hand. Taiho remained almost at his fighting weight of 330 pounds after his retirement and Dr Hayashi said that excess weight had been a direct cause of the stroke.

Weight loss on retirement is important, then, but it must be done with care. Former grand champion Kitanofuji (now Kokonoe Oyakata and Chiyonofuji's and Hokutoumi's stablemaster) suffered a mild heart attack by trying to reduce too rapidly after retiring in 1974. Taiho's main rival in the 1960s, former yokozuna Kashiwado, took off about 50 kilograms over a five-year period to cope with his diabetes, with no ill effects. Ex-yokozuna Takanosato (now Naruto Oyakata) even wrote a book about how he brought his diabetes under control while he was an active grand champion.

THE SUMO SCHOOL

Sumo school, or *kyoshujo,* is located on the second floor of the Kokugikan. It includes a classroom as well as a large training area that contains three sumo rings. All new sumo apprentices are required to attend the school for the first six months of their sumo career.

Here they are taught the basic training exercises as well as ring techniques and tactics. Classroom courses include lessons in anatomy, sumo history, calligraphy and traditional singing. At the same time they must learn to recite from memory the 11-point Sumo Creed that begins 'Carry yourself with pride at all times because you are a rikishi in Japan's national sport of sumo.' Although rikishi may not consciously claim to be the modern-day equivalent of the samurai, the fact remains that they are following a strict set of principles similar to those that formed the famed *bushido* code of the Japanese warrior.

Before the start of each daily classroom session, the young sumo students stand and recite the creed in unison, reminding themselves that 'sumo begins and ends with courtesy, not only on the dohyo but in your daily life as well'. It also enjoins them to 'behave like a flower of the people and refrain from doing anything that shows a lack of public morality and common sense'.

Where do they find such fine young men who are ready to dedicate themselves to such a rugged, disciplined life with only a slim chance of success? Each stable has its own team of scouts scouring the villages and towns for new recruits. Many of these scouts are former rikishi who work part-time tracking down talented youngsters, always with the dream of discovering a potential star. The masters and training coaches of the various stables also keep their eyes open for promising juniors during the jungyo tours of the rural areas and the

smaller cities between the six official tournaments. College and amateur sumo champions are also the objects of fierce competition among sumo stables, particularly since the example of former *gakusei* (student) yokozuna Wajima, who went all the way to the top in professional sumo in 1973. No less than a dozen stables vied for two recent college champions, Kushima and Yamazaki, with Dewanoumi Beya recruiting the former and Tatsunami Beya the latter.

Experts maintain that the scout must scrutinize the feet of the new recruit with particular care. The bigger his feet, the greater a youth's chances of someday making yokozuna. The feet of the great former yokozuna, Taiho, reportedly continued to grow right up to the time he retired at the age of 31. The feet are important perhaps because they tend to anchor the rikishi to the dohyo and allow him to dig in at the edge. Also, because they reach their full size before the rest of the body, they can indicate that if the recruit has big feet, he will surely have a big body when he finishes growing. (Others use similar logic with refer-

ence to significantly large hands.)

The students at sumo school start off the day with a few laps around the Kokugikan. Then comes a series of traditional exercises, beginning with an hour of *shiko,* or foot stamping. This means alternately lifting up each leg as high as it will go and then stamping down hard on the clay surface to strengthen the hips and legs. Shiko is followed by 15 minutes or so of squatting, then *shinkaku* – extending each leg alternately from a squatting position and bending forward in the direction of the leg; and *teppo* – slapping a wooden pole hundreds of times, while rhythmically moving one's feet backward and forward.

These exercises limber up the students for the tough *matawari* – the sumo splits exercise. This is the exercise that brought tears to the eyes of Hawaiian Jesse Kuhaulua, who fought under the name of Takamiyama, as well as to the Tongans who fought in sumo for about a year in the late 1970s. It typifies the remorseless self-punishment that a young hopeful must endure if he wants to get to the top.

New recruits have to spend the first six months of their life in professional sumo at the Sumo School run by and within the Kokugikan. Here they learn the rules, etiquette, basic techniques and sumo history; the feeling in the school is more or less that of a technological high school or polytechnic.

CLASH OF THE GIANTS

CHIYONOFUJI VERSUS ONOKUNI

As the two rugged, powerfully built sumo grand champions (yokozuna) crouch like coiled springs opposite each other in the centre of the ring glaring fiercely at one another, a growing tension fills the arena. Eleven thousand Japanese spectators lean foward expectantly, waiting for the final bout of the tournament to begin, many shouting out their allegiance to their favourite wrestler. The timekeeper raises his hand to indicate that the four-minute, pre-bout ritual is over and the match is about to begin. Chiyonofuji takes a handful of salt to throw into the centre of the dohyo in a Shinto rite of purification.

Unusually light for a grand champion at 6 feet, 270 pounds, the 33-year-old Chiyonofuji resembles more a muscular body-builder than a typical sumo wrestler. He is a marked contrast to his massive opponent, Onokuni, who is almost the stereotyped image of the tradi-

tional roly-poly sumo wrestler. At 26, Onokuni stands just over 6 feet 2 inches and weighing in at a prodigious 448 pounds, he is the second heaviest in professional sumo. His huge, protruding belly belies his great strength, however. One need only realize that for the past 11 years he has been enduring, indeed thriving upon, some of the toughest, most gruelling training of any athlete anywhere in the world today.

The prize money of $4,000 that's on the line for this bout is not the motivating force in this electric atmosphere. A place in history is more important. Chiyonofuji has been on a historic run of 53 consecutive wins and has his sights set on the all-time record of 69 wins in a row set in the late 1930s. If he can continue to dominate Onokuni as he has been doing in the past and wins this final bout of the Kyushu Tournament, he can equal that seemingly invincible record two months from

Left and below
Chiyonofuji and Onokuni carry out the preliminaries, going back for salt, crouching down at the shikiri-sen (white lines which demarcate their sides of the dohyo) and glaring at each other defiantly. Chiyonfuji has by far the greater number of victories in encounters so far, Onokuni has much more weight and strength, and in a sense he has nothing to lose. Chiyonofuji is supremely confident in his ability to beat all-comers, as he has done for the previous 50 or so bouts, and is seemingly unstoppable.

Below The tachiai. Chiyonofuji fights only on the belt and is extremely quick, often getting his left hand on the belt within the first couple of seconds of a bout, after which it is almost impossible to dislodge him or make him break his grip. He then uses his agility and strength to get even much larger opponents like Onokuni and Konishiki off balance so that he can throw them, or into a position where he can muscle them out of the ring. Onokuni fights both on the belt and by thrusting and pushing. Chiyonofuji keeps his belt very tight, though, and it is often difficult, even for someone as strong as Onokuni, to get a grip on it, so the initial charge is all important.

now on the final day of the New Year's Tournament in January if he remains unbeaten. Onokuni has won only seven of their previous 26 bouts and has won a mere three championships (*yusho*) compared to Chiyonofuji's 26 – second-best to the all-time record total of 32 yusho set by the great Taiho, who dominated sumo in the 1960s. And to make matters worse, Onokuni has been unable to beat Chiyo in over a year. But Onokuni has pledged himself to upset the odds and win that bout, even though Chiyonofuji has already clinched the tournament title the day before.

The referee raises his war-fan as a signal for the long-awaited jump-off, the two yokozuna instantly spring up from their crouching position and crash into each other. The bout has begun! Onokuni moves with surprising speed at the jump-off, immediately seizing Chiyonofuji's belt with his left hand in a move that takes Chiyo unawares and proves decisive in the end. Chiyonofuji is able to get his right hand inside on the belt in a *migi-yotsu* position, but Onokuni's left-handed grip squeezes Chiyo's right arm in tight so that he can't exert his full power on that side. Chiyonofuji whirls Onokuni around in an effort to dislodge his left hand from the belt, but the Big Panda hangs on tenaciously and quickly regains the offensive. And before Chiyonofuji can launch another counter-attack, Onokuni bulldozes him to the edge, then releases his belt grip and drives a tremendous left-handed thrust against Chiyo's neck and sends the great man tumbling over backwards out of the ring. The Fukuoka arena erupts with a huge roar as the spectators leap to their feet, some sending seat cushions sailing toward the dohyo in a bewildered mixture of shock, excitement and delight. With his scintillating and courageous display, Onokuni has abruptly ended

fellow-yokozuna Chiyonofuji's 53-bout unbeaten run, the second-longest winning streak in modern sumo history! This had to be one of the great moments of this fascinating sport, full of the thrills and emotion and brilliantly deployed power that all sumo fans thirst for.

Far left Onokuni has released his grip on Chiyonofuni's belt, but still has a lock on his elbow. Note Chiyonofuji's lower centre of gravity, which he has often used to great advantage in other bouts.

Left Within seconds Chiyonofuji has been forced to the edge and is falling. With Onokuni on top of him. The impossible has happened. For Onokuni this was the moment that restored his confidence in himself and made him look like a Grand Champion again, after too many poor tournaments. For Chiyonofuji it was proof that nobody is invincible, although he did have the satisfaction of knowing that he had gone down to another Grand Champion.

GLOSSARY

Abisetaoshi Backward force-down
Anma Massage; sekitori wrestling with lower-ranked rikishi in practice
Banzuke Ranking list issued 13 days before each basho
Basho Tournament; there are six basho held on the odd months of every year, each lasting 15 days
Bintsuke Grease used for arranging the rikishi's topknot
Butsukari-geiko Last phase of daily training
Chanko-nabe Traditional boiled stew, usually containing vegetables, chicken, pork, or fish; the staple diet of the wrestlers
Chaya Traditional teahouses that handle most of the choice boxes at the Kokugikan, and provide refreshments for customers using such boxes
Chiho-Sewanin Scouts who search for prospective rikishi
Chiri-chozu Part of the rikishi's ritual before each bout
Chon-mage Top-knot style used by rikishi ranked in Makushita and below, and by rikishi in the top two divisions on informal occasions
Danpatsu-shiki Hair-cutting ceremony for retiring rikishi
Deshi Any rikishi in a stable
Dohyo Sumo ring
Dohyo-iri Ring-entering ceremony by Juryo and Makunouchi rikishi, and by yokozuna
Dohyo-matsuri Ring-purifying ceremony held the day before each basho
Fundoshi Loin cloth worn under the kesho-mawashi, or by rikishi waiting in the shitaku-beya for their bout
Gino-sho Technique Prize
Gunbai War fan carried by the referee
Gunbai-dori Agreement with referee's decision after a mono-ii
Gyoji Referee
Hana-zumo Sumo show, including one-day exhibition tournament.
Hatakikomi Slap-down
Heya (or beya) Sumo stable
Hidari Left-hand or -sided
Higashi East
Hikiotoshi Hand pull-down
Hikkake Arm-grabbing force-out
Ichimon Group of related stables
Isu-seki Single balcony seats
Intai-zumo Retirement ceremony

Jikan-ippai 'Time is up': the signal for the two rikishi to prepare to wrestle
Jinku Traditional sumo songs
Jonidan Fifth and largest division in sumo
Jonokuchi Sixth and lowest division in sumo
Jungyo Rural tours between tournaments
Juryo The second sumo division (the lowest at which a salary is paid)
Kachi-koshi Rikishi achieving a majority of victories during a basho: eight wins for sekitori and four for lower-ranked rikishi
Kanji Chinese script used for Japanese writing
Kanreki Dohyo-iri Ceremony in which the yokozuna dohyo-iri is performed when a former yokozuna reaches his 60th birthday
Kanto-sho Fighting Spirit Prize
Keikoba Practice-bout area in a stable
Ken-sho Special prizes awarded to the winner of a bout, usually found only in Makunouchi
Kesho-mawashi Embroidered silk apron worn by sekitori
Ketaguri Foot-sweep technique
Kimura Shonosuke Traditional name given the top-ranked referee
Kinboshi Gold star in the form of money awarded to maegashira rikishi who defeat a Grand Champion, provided they get kachi-koshi
Koenkai Supporting associations that help to finance stables as well as individual rikishi ranked in Makuuchi and Juryo
Kokugikan National Sumo Arena in Tokyo
Komusubi Fourth-highest rank in Makunouchi
Kotenage Arm-lock throw
Kyoshujo Sumo school
Mae-bukuro Belt area covering the vital organs; grabbing an opponent in this area leads to automatic disqualification
Maegashira Lowest level of Makunouchi
Mae-zumo Pre-sumo or the qualifying class in sumo, the lowest rung on the ladder
Make-koshi Minority; applied to a lower-ranked rikishi who loses at least four bouts or a sekitori who loses at least eight bouts in a basho

Makunouchi 'Inside the curtain': the first division in sumo
Masu-seki Boxes on the main floor of a sumo arena, usually seating four
Matawari Sumo splits – a sometimes painful leg-stretching exercise
Matta 'Not ready!': the call of a rikishi on the dohyo who is not yet ready to commence wrestling when his opponent starts to launch his attack
Mawashi Rikishi's belt
Migi Right-handed or -sided
Mono-ii Judge's conference, held if a judge(s) disagrees with a gyoji's decision
Montuski Crested kimono worn by sekitori on formal occasions
Nishi West
Oicho-mage Ginko-leaf style hair-do of sekitori
Okamisan Stablemaster's wife
Okuridashi Rear push-out
Okuritaoshi Rear push-down
Oshitaoshi Frontal push-down
Oshi-zumo Pushing style of sumo
Oyakata Officials of the Sumo Kyokai following retirement from active sumo careers
Ozeki Champion: the second-highest-ranked rikishi of the Makunouchi Division
Rikishi Sumo wrestler
Sanban-geiko Series of practice bouts between two sekitori
Sandanme Fourth division on the banzuke
Sansho Three special prizes awarded at the end of each basho to Makunouchi rikishi below ozeki
Sanyaku Ranks above maegashira: komusubi, sekiwake, ozeki and yokozuna
Sanyaku Soroibumi Ring-entering ritual at end of last day of a basho, involving the top-ranked rikishi competing in the final three bouts in Makunouchi
Sashi-chigai Referee's decision overturned by the judges after a mono-ii
Sekitori Rikishi ranked in sumo's two top divisions
Sekiwake Third-highest rank in Makunouchi
Senshuraku Final day of a basho
Sewanin Ex-rikishi, usually ex-Juryo or ex-Makushita, who work for the Sumo Kyokai

Shikimori Inosuke Traditional name given the second-highest ranked referee

Shikiri Salt-tossing preliminary before each bout

Shiko Foot-stamping training to strengthen the hips and legs

Shikona Rikishi's fighting name

Shimekomi Silk belt worn by sekitori, usually called mawashi

Shimpan Judge

Shinkyaku Leg-stretching exercise

Shiranui-Gata One of the two styles of the yokozuna ring-entering ceremony

Shitatenage Under-arm throw

Shukun-sho Outstanding Performance Award given for upsetting yokozuna

Shussei-hiro Introduction ritual on the eighth day of a basho for new recruits who have passed through mae-zumo

Sotogake Outside leg trip

Sumo-ji Kanji script unique to the sumo world

Sumo Kyokai Sumo's governing body (officially, it is Nihon Sumo Kyokai)

Sumotori Alternative name for rikishi

Tachi-ai Initial charge at the start of a bout

Tachimochi Swordbearer for yokozuna during his dohyo-iri

Tate-gyoji Chief referee

Tegata Signed handprint of a rikishi

Tenno-shihai Emperor's Cup awarded to the Makunouchi yusho winner at each basho

Teppo Wooden pole which rikishi slap to strengthen their hands

Tokoyama Hairdresser

Tori-naoshi Rematch called by the judges after a mono-ii

Toshiyori Retired name for rikishi remaining in the Sumo Kyokai

Toshiyori kabu Retired, elder's name involving stock in Sumo Kyokai, usually costing at least three-quarters of a million dollars

Tsukebito Rikishi in Makushita or the lower divisions serving as an attendant to a sekitori

Tsukidashi Thrust-out

Tsukitaoshi Thrust-down

Tsukiotoshi Twist-down

Tsuna White hawser worn by yokozuna during their dohyo-iri that is also a symbol of their rank

Tsuppari Thrusting tactics

Tsuridashi Lift-out

Tsuriotoshi Lift-dump

Tsuyuharai Herald for yokozuna during the dohyo-iri

Uchigake Inside leg trip

Unryu-Gata One of two yokozuna ring-entering ceremonies

Utchari Backward pivot throw

Uwatenage Over-arm throw

Wakamono-gashira Ex-rikishi, usually ex-Juryo or Makushita, who manage younger rikishi in a stable

Yagura Wooden frame tower outside sumo arenas on top of which yobidashi beat a drum at the end of each day's bouts

Yokozuna Highest and only permanent rank in sumo

Yorikiri Frontal force-out

Yoritaoshi Frontal crush-out

Yotsu-zumo Belt-fighting style of sumo

Yumitori-shiki Bow-twirling ceremony at end of each day's final bout

Zensho-yusho Perfect championship accomplished by winning every bout

INDEX

80